ADVANCED VENTURA

George Sheldon

MIS: PRESS

MANAGEMENT INFORMATION SOURCE, INC.

COPYRIGHT

1107 N.W. 14th Avenue
Portland, Oregon 97209
(503) 222-2399

First Printing

ISBN 0-943518-81-4

Library of Congress Catalog Card Number: 88-2062

TRADEMARKS

DEDICATION

For Gloria, of course.

She believed, when others — even I — wondered.

ACKNOWLEDGMENTS

I want to especially thank Annie M. Barfuss, one of the Account Executives at Hill & Knowlton. No matter what my request, Annie was always there.

Thanks also to Kim Anne Thomas and Bob Williams at MIS: Press for their support and help, and for believing in this project from the very beginning.

Special thanks to Donald R. Pollard, Sally A. Sheetz, and Bob Wray for their advice, support, and help—no matter how busy they were when I asked hundreds of questions.

I also want to thank all the companies and their personnel who so graciously provided me with copies of their software, loaned me hardware, and supplied information about their products. The list is long, and I appreciate everyone's help and support.

I also thank Mark Leaser at Office Works in Lancaster, Pennsylvania for making hardware available to me on a moment's notice so I could keep working on this book.

And last but far from least, with deep, warm, heart-filled appreciation, special thanks to Charles Byrd because without him in the beginning, where would I be today?

TABLE OF CONTENTS

FOREWORD

This book was written in WordPerfect 4.2. The text was cleaned, edited, and criticized by both RightWriter and Grammatik II. The text was then forwarded to the publisher via diskette, and the publisher used Ventura to prepare the final page composition.

Many of the illustrations were created with Ventura Publisher. Some of the art was prepared on a Macintosh, and other pieces were enhanced with the assistance of Publisher's Paintbrush. Some manual pasting was also performed to form the final pages before this book was sent to the printer. Various laser printers were used to print the type and illustrations. Some type, such as large headlines, was produced by commercial typesetting methods and manually pasted into position.

To the best of the author's knowledge and belief, there really is no Pennsylvania Food Corporation or Pennsylvania Snack Food Corporation. These fictitious companies, as well as the Twister Snack, were created solely for editorial content for this book. Neither the author nor the publisher intended these illustrations to be anything other than editorial comments, and the illustrations were not intended to represent any company, firm, product, or business from the past, present, or future. Any resemblance to any existing enterprise is purely coincidental and certainly not intended.

Finally, there really is a Jollie Mollie (real name, Mollie Ethel). Yes, she is available to do TV commercials, should anyone be interested. Perhaps, finally, she can start earning her keep around one writer's house here in south central Pennsylvania.

George Sheldon
Mt. Joy, Pennsylvania
April, 1988

CHAPTER 1

DESKTOP PUBLISHING: AN INTRODUCTION

The term **desktop publishing** was coined by Paul Brainerd, founder of Aldus Corporation — the company that produces PageMaker page-composition software. Often called "the father of desktop publishing," Brainerd took his idea — producing typeset-quality documents on a personal computer — to then Apple chief Steve Jobs. Jobs loved the idea, and the rest is history.

Just as Paul Brainerd, Steve Jobs, and the Macintosh started desktop publishing as it is known today, Xerox Ventura Publisher brought desktop publishing to PC- and MS-DOS machines.

Desktop publishing originated on the Macintosh because of the Macintosh's rich graphics environment. There are many estimates of how many desktop publishers exist. Thousands use Macintosh computers; others use IBM (or compatible) PC- or MS-DOS computers. Some use a combination of both.

First introduced in the fall of 1986, Ventura Publisher was among the first true desktop publishing packages designed for business users. Developed by Ventura Software, Inc. and marketed exclusively by the Xerox Corporation, the first release of the product was widely acclaimed as the best PC-DOS- and MS-DOS desktop publishing product available. For some of those millions of PC-DOS and MS-DOS-based computer users, Ventura offered true desktop publishing.

Ventura's compatibility with many leading software packages — including widely used and installed word processors and graphics products — is one reason it was broadly accepted. Because of the large installed base of IBM computers, Ventura quickly found a niche. Its compatibility with IBM-based hardware and software was wanted — and demanded — by potential desktop publishers.

Ventura's ease of use — including point-and-click mouse control — was quickly accepted as a standard for all desktop publishing software. Ventura's style sheets offered users instant control over documents. By being able to place text into a predetermined format, IBM-based computer users were able to begin desktop publishing without much additional expense.

Desktop publishing software is page-composition software. The ability to mix graphics and text and place this combination in a specific, defined way on the page is the purpose of desktop publishing. Ventura does all this and more.

Again, desktop publishing involves using a personal computer to prepare camera-ready documents for reproduction or publication. **Camera-ready** means your document is typeset; line drawings are positioned properly; and photographs are included in the finished, printed form. Camera-ready also means that the document need only be photographed by the printer so a printing plate can be made. Copies of your document can then be printed in any quantity.

Many of your documents will be reproduced by a printer—usually on an offset printing press. Some jobs (small quantities, usually fewer than 50) are often reproduced on a high-quality photocopying machine. Regardless of mass-reproduction techniques, the goal of desktop publishing is to produce camera-ready documents that need only be handed to a printer or photocopier operator with instructions of how many copies to print and how you want them bound.

Throughout this book, it is assumed that as a desktop publisher you want to reproduce or publish your documents. Again, the objective is not to produce a single document (although as a desktop publisher you are creating one document—the master), but to produce many copies of the same document. Unless you own a printing press—and few people do—you will require printing services. The goal, then, is to use your computer and Ventura to create documents to be published by your printing service.

ADVANTAGES OF DESKTOP PUBLISHING

There are three main advantages to using desktop publishing instead of conventional printing methods:

- **Speed.** Within minutes, you can produce camera-ready documents. Before desktop publishing, you sent documents to a typesetter and waited until they were ready—perhaps weeks later. To make changes in type size, you sent the job back to the typesetter and, again, waited for your work to be ready for pickup.

- **Control.** With desktop publishing, you have total control over the final appearance of the document. You can choose the size and style of your type and even the size of your line art and drawings.

- **Cost.** Typesetting services, paste-up boards, press-on type, and rule lines add production costs to each document. By using a personal computer to produce camera-ready documents, you eliminate these costs. Although the system can be expensive—and supplies for a laser printer are *not* free—within a short period of time, your desktop publishing system can save you money.

The advantages of desktop publishing are complementary. For example, suppose you produce an annual report. Last year, it was published by traditional methods: it was handed to a printer and, a month later, delivered with a hefty bill.

During that month, the printer supplied you with proofs. Even if you weren't entirely happy with the layout, you may have decided to accept it because if you decided to change it, you would have increased the typesetting cost and delayed the final delivery date.

This year, the annual report is due, but you will create it with Ventura and your desktop publishing system. When data for your document is ready, you can import it into Ventura. Within minutes, you will see how your finished report will look.

Suppose you'd like to see a different layout. A few mouse clicks and moments later, the new design appears on the screen. There is no cost to see the difference in design, and it takes only a few moments.

After design decisions are made, the document can be printed on a laser printer for final review and proofing. If satisfactory, the camera-ready document can then be sent to the printer for printing.

What took a month the year before now takes only days. The time the printer requires to print the final document remains the same, but the time to complete the typesetting is eliminated. The document will be in the form you want rather than in the form someone else thought you wanted. Printing costs remain the same, but charges for traditional typesetting and changes are eliminated.

LEVELS OF DESKTOP PUBLISHING

There are three levels of desktop publishing.

The first level is the beginner's stage of desktop publishing. Such desktop publishers are just a step above using a word processor to produce documents. Desktop publishers in the beginner's stage use low-end page composition software and perhaps a dot-matrix printer for output. The work they produce is only suitable for the local scout troop or internal documents in a business, such as company picnic notices.

Second-level desktop publishers often refer to themselves as desktop publishers, but a better term is "word publishers." Using a better word processor—such as WordPerfect, WordStar, or Microsoft Word—and using a laser printer, these desktop publishers simply produce fancy printing. Instead of using a daisy-wheel or dot-matrix printer, they use a laser printer for outstanding output. Many of these documents will not be mass-produced, but a single copy will be used for correspondence or a memo. When a "word publishing" document is mass-produced, it is usually reproduced with a photocopy machine.

At the third level of desktop publishing are true desktop publishers. They use a page-composition program such as Ventura to set camera-ready pages. They use laser printers for output and often use a service bureau for higher-resolution output. Desktop publishers use scanners, clip art libraries, paint-and-draw programs, and digitized images to create documents for mass-production. The quantity needed determines how the final document will be printed for distribution.

DESKTOP PUBLISHING PROBLEMS

Desktop publishers encounter many problems. Laser printer output may prove inadequate for documents that were previously sent to a printer for mass-production. For example, if a magazine was previously produced with traditional typesetting methods but is now prepared for printing with laser printer output, in most cases, the results will be unsatisfactory.

If, on the other hand, a document was previously produced on a typewriter and will now be produced by a desktop publisher on a laser printer, the result will usually be more than acceptable.

The required use of photos, line art, and even special logos and typefaces in your finished documents also determine your course of action as a desktop publisher.

In any case, desktop publishing output should be equal to or better than that produced by previous production methods. The goal is to never stop improving the appearance of documents.

VENTURA PUBLISHER DOES IT ALL

Just as there are several different levels of desktop publishing, there are different levels of Ventura use. You may need only to produce simple documents, and the standard style sheets provided with Ventura may meet all your needs.

Because Ventura is relatively simple to begin using, many users become fooled into thinking it cannot be pushed farther. Actually, one of the best features of Ventura is that it can be used on many different levels.

The purpose of this book is to move you—the true desktop publisher—from beginning to advanced Ventura use. Many solutions to your problems can be found in this book; others must wait for tomorrow's technology.

ABOUT THE BOOK

As the name implies, *Advanced Ventura* is not intended for beginners. Other books teach you step-by-step how to operate Ventura; this book demonstrates how Ventura can be used to create professional documents. You will be provided with tips, hints, information, and guidelines to help you use Ventura at the highest level. If you already know how to operate Ventura, this book should help expand your knowledge of how to use this versatile program.

If you are not yet comfortable with Ventura and the general concepts of desktop publishing, you should first learn the basics of Ventura and then return to this book.

The Jollie Mollie Ad Campaign

In Appendix B, as well as in figures throughout the book, the Jollie Mollie Advertising campaign—a fictional report created for a nonexistent company—will be used for illustration purposes. This report—as originally prepared on a word processor—is presented at the end of the book so you can see how you can create a complete, professional-looking report by using Ventura.

CHAPTER 2

BUILDING YOUR DESKTOP PUBLISHING SYSTEM

With Ventura Publisher, you can create manuals, books, magazines, reports, brochures, pamphlets, and almost any other regularly published document. As you continue to use Ventura, you will see that it does not limit your capability to publish your own documents; rather, the limits of your own imagination, intuitiveness, and ingenuity determine how far you progress.

Becoming a desktop publisher involves more than just operating a page-composition program such as Ventura. Desktop publishers are required to operate many different programs—word processors, paint-and-draw programs, and utilities—and create documents.

Although Ventura is a powerful page-composition program, there are certain tasks it cannot perform. It is recommended that you only use Ventura as a page-composition program and use other programs to accomplish other tasks.

For example, you could type text directly in Ventura, but Ventura does not provide all the same editing tools as do today's word processors. You should use a word processor to perform word-processing tasks and Ventura to perform desktop publishing tasks.

To be an effective desktop publisher and use Ventura to its fullest potential, you must incorporate several other programs. Because Ventura is the keystone of your desktop publishing system, additional software products must be compatible with Ventura.

The learning path starts with DOS and moves into word processing, paint-and-draw programs, and finally Ventura. For example, if you plan to publish documents containing Lotus 1-2-3 spreadsheet data, you should probably learn to operate Lotus 1-2-3. You may not need to know the program in detail, but you will need to know how to create, edit, revise, and print a simple spreadsheet.

The following section outlines what certain software and hardware products can do and how they can be of value to the desktop publisher. Although other, similar products may be available, based on the author's reviews, these products work effectively with Ventura as part of a total desktop publishing system.

WORD PROCESSORS

Several word processors are recommended for use with Ventura. WordPerfect tops the list; its ease of use, merge and macro features, and ability to quickly and easily assemble documents—combined with the WordPerfect Corporation's toll-free technical support—make this program the Cadillac of word processors. A close second is Microsoft Word. If you love to use the mouse, Microsoft Word is for you, although you can use it without a mouse. Word provides all the standard features of today's word processors and offers additional advanced features, including a strong spelling dictionary and an on-line thesaurus.

If WordPerfect is the Cadillac of word processors, Microsoft Word is the Lincoln Continental. Your decision between WordPerfect and Microsoft Word might be similar to deciding which of these two cars to purchase and drive. The most important thing to remember is that the word processor you choose will be used often, and, accordingly, you should "test-drive" any package before you buy. Compare, test, and decide which program is best for you.

Don't forget that to become a proficient desktop publisher, you must first be a proficient word processing operator. Whatever word processing program you choose, do whatever it takes—schools, books, training seminars—to learn as much about it as you can.

Other word processors are worthy of consideration. WordStar—at one time the leading word processing program—fell flat for a while. With one of the most recognized names in the computer industry, WordStar is beginning to again battle for the market share it once held. The latest version reviewed—WordStar Professional Release 4—includes many improvements over early WordStar releases. WordStar includes WordFinder, an on-line thesaurus.

Other word processors that work with Ventura are DisplayWrite 3 and DisplayWrite 4, MultiMate, Xerox Writer, and XyWrite. Any other word processor that can save your documents in ASCII text can be used with Ventura.

Make sure your word processor has a strong spell-checker and an on-line thesaurus. It should also have block move, copy, and delete functions, an undo feature, and the ability to create and reuse macros. Above all, make sure you can import the text it produces into Ventura.

If you are not now using a powerful word processor, consider upgrading.

Word Processor Add-ons

Although today's word processors offer many powerful features, there are still some tasks that can only be completed by add-on features.

Grammar and Style Checkers

One such add-on that all desktop publishers need is a grammar and style checker. Using principles of artificial intelligence, these programs analyze sentence structure and offer suggestions for improving your writing. These style checkers also look for other typing inconsistencies, such as missing quotation marks, unmatched use of parentheses, and errors in capitalization. Missing punctuation is also marked.

One problem with grammar and style checkers is that they occasionally flag phrases as possible problems when nothing is actually wrong. Also, they are not always able to read for context. Even with such annoyances, however, they are worth their weight in gold. They will search, find, and report errors and make you more aware of your writing.

Two grammar and style checkers are highly recommended—RightWriter and Grammatik II. Both programs are easy to learn, and they perform very well. Grammatik II offers more analysis of your overall document, while RightWriter seems a bit more critical of writing style and offers more suggestions for improvement. The latest versions of these two programs are greatly improved over earlier releases. Because of the comparison characteristics of the programs (they compare your writing with standards established in their files), they take time to run, but both programs run within acceptable time ranges, and the time is well spent.

No desktop publisher should be without one of these programs. Before buying a grammar- and style-checking program, make sure it is compatible with your word processor.

Chapter 3 discusses how to make your word processor work harder, which makes Ventura easier to use.

Word Processing Utility Programs

If you will be receiving text from other computer users who may be using a word processor other than the one you are using, WordforWord is a program you should consider adding to your desktop publishing system. WordforWord is a conversion program that quickly and easily converts one word processing format to another. For example, you can change a document from WordStar to WordPerfect format. Many different combinations are available in WordforWord; it is a well-behaved program and is highly recommended. Before purchasing, make sure it will convert formatted documents to the word processor you will be using. If you are using standard, popular word processing software, WordforWord can do the job.

CompareRite is another superb word processing utility; it checks your revisions and provides redline and automatic strike-out features. It works quickly and is compatible with most word processing programs. If you work in an environment where your documents undergo a series of revisions, edits, and reviews before being published, CompareRite can keep track of each edited version.

DISK UTILITY PROGRAMS

Desktop publishing without a hard disk will make you wish you never heard of computing. Because of the large amount of storage needed to operate a desktop publishing system, you will need a hard disk. There are several excellent utility programs to make it easier to use a computer with a hard disk.

Norton Utilities 4.0 Advanced Edition should be in your toolbox. Its now-famous Undelete program alone makes it worth the price. Other utilities—such as Speed Disk and Text Search—make this program a bargain. If you do not yet own a copy, it should be on your shopping list.

SuperKey and SideKick are also effective utility programs. SuperKey is an excellent macro programming tool that permits you to run programs and eliminate repetitive keystrokes. SideKick includes a Note function that allows you to import portions of text from one document to another—even text from different programs. Using both SideKick and SuperKey is like having an invisible third hand while using your word-processing program. Ventura's reference guide, however, issues a warning against using Sidekick when running Ventura. The manual reports that Ventura's performance is degraded and, most importantly, SideKick's and Ventura's graphics are not compatible. This problem can cause data loss and give you unpredictable results. There is no warning issued about SuperKey; however, because SuperKey is a macro program, and much work in Ventura is mouse-oriented, the usefulness of having SuperKey in RAM is questionable when running Ventura. While these two programs probably should not be in RAM while Ventura is running, these programs are excellent additions for the word processing stages of desktop publishing.

GRAPHICS SOFTWARE

If Ventura has one weakness, it is its limited graphics capabilities. If you will be publishing documents with many graphics, you will soon find the internal graphics ability of Ventura inadequate.

The best way to overcome this inadequacy is to add a graphics package to your desktop publishing tool kit. Fortunately, many excellent graphics, painting, and drawing programs are available.

Chapter 4 discusses in detail information about graphics and graphics programs, including GEM Presentation Team, Microsoft Windows, Micrografx Windows Draw and Windows Graph, ZSoft's Publisher's Paintbrush, and Halo DPE.

THE HARDWARE JUNGLE

A big, fancy, 80386-chip computer is not necessary for most desktop publishing. Many programs mentioned in this book were tested on an 8088-chip computer with a 20-megabyte hard disk and 640K RAM—the equivalent of an IBM XT—to ensure that they work with relativley low-end hardware.

The 80286 chip, however, is nudging the old 8088 chip out of use. Computers with this chip—the IBM AT standard—are most commonly purchased.

If you are planning to buy a computer, consider the 80386-chip machines. It may be well worth the additional $1,000 investment, especially if your computer will be used exclusively for desktop publishing. A computer equipped with an 80286 chip, however, can probably do everything you will need (but a bit more slowly).

In summary, 80386-based machines are probably best for extensive, heavy use. You can use an 80286-based machine, but it will take longer to do your work. In theory, you can use an 8088-based machine, but you'll find it too slow to do real work. Buy at least an 80286 machine or an 80386 machine if you can afford it.

The more RAM your computer contains, the better. 512K RAM is standard, but if you can upgrade to 640K RAM by adding chips, do so. If you are fortunate enough to have one megabyte of RAM, you will find it worthwhile.

Also, you *must* have a hard disk, and the standard 20 megabytes may not be enough. Forty megabytes seems adequate, but if you will be publishing many graphics or scanned images, you might find 40 megabytes inadequate. Consider a 60- or 70-megabyte hard drive if you are a full-time desktop publisher and use many graphics.

The computer's brand name does not matter as long as it runs PC- or MS-DOS, includes at least a 20-megabyte hard disk, and contains 640K RAM.

Laser Printers

Chapter 6 explores laser printers, why you need one, and their limitations. PostScript printers and Hewlett-Packard Printer Command Language printers are discussed.

Scanners

Chapter 5 explores scanners and their limitations.

Big Screen Monitors

Reasons for choosing a big-screen monitor include the ability to view two side-by-side pages and the ability to view one full page.

For example, the monochrome monitor made by Princeton Graphic Systems — the LM-301 — sports a 15" screen, four shades of gray, and a resolution of 1664 (H) × 1200 (V) pixels. The actual screen display is 11" wide and 8-1/2" high, which will display your pages one-half their actual height. If you must have a true full-page screen, Princeton's LM-300 will do the job. If you are not producing side-by-side pages — documents such as directories, reports, parts catalogs, or similar single-sheet jobs — the LM-300 will be adequate. It offers the same resolution as the LM-301.

If you want a big-screen color monitor, consider Moniterm's Viking, a giant 19" monitor. While big-screen monitors are expensive, they will make your work much easier.

The higher resolution of big-screen monitors requires that you install a controller board. To avoid mismatches and optimize performance, use controller boards offered by the monitor manufacturers. There are hundreds of thousands of pixels on big-screen monitors. (On extra-large screens, there can be over three million pixels.)

The Mouse

Although you can operate Ventura without a mouse, you probably never will; it takes too much time. The Microsoft Mouse or the Logitech Mouse will do the job. There are other mice available; just make sure the one you choose fits in your hand and is comfortable to operate.

Communications

Modems

To send files via telephone to a service bureau, you will also need a modem. Choose at least a 1200-baud modem; the higher speed permits you to send four times as much information. Microstuf's Crosstalk Mk.4 can easily do the job for you; its automatic scripts take the work out of connecting to a typesetting service bureau. See Chapter 15 for more information about service bureaus and transmitting files.

Fax Modems

If your business is across town, in the next state, or across the country from someone who must send you text, pictures, or graphics, a facsimile (fax) modem is the answer. After you install a fax modem board in your computer, anyone with a fax machine can send you documents. The main difference between a fax modem and a regular modem is the ability to receive and send graphics. Fax modems convert text and images into fax format and operate at speeds of 9600 baud.

The Cost

Many desktop publishers are already computer users; therefore, they own some of the system already, such as the computer, monitor, word processor, and hard disk.

A low-end desktop publishing system costs $3,500-$5,000 and includes an IBM-compatible computer, mouse, monitor, CGA or EGA graphics board, and a low-priced laser printer. A complete, advanced system including a PostScript printer, an 80386-based computer, a scanner, modem, big-screen monitor, and software can cost between $12,500 and $17,500.

After buying hardware, you need to have enough left to buy a decent word processor and, of course, Ventura. After purchasing the laser printer and Ventura, you can add software for graphics and text preparation and perhaps a few more pieces of hardware, such as a scanner and controller board for a laser printer.

Look for package deals. Many dealers offer packaged systems at reduced prices.

YOUR SYSTEM AND VENTURA

One of Ventura's true benefits is that it can be used with so many other computer products. With rare exceptions, Ventura can be used with most hardware configurations and software programs associated with desktop publishing. You can always expand, add, modify, and change your desktop publishing system as your abilities and publishing needs grow.

CHAPTER 3

WORD PROCESSING POWER

Ventura Publisher is a powerful page-composition program, but it is not a word processor. The important point to remember is that your word processor, not Ventura, should be used to create your text.

If you are not using a powerful word processor, such as WordPerfect, Microsoft Word, or WordStar, you may want to consider upgrading now. Your word processor should at least include a spell checker and an on-line thesaurus for editing.

If you or your staff members have never taken the time to learn how to use the many features of your word processor, now is the time to begin that task. It is not so much which word processor you have but using that word processor to its full potential that counts. Ventura's ability to import text from virtually any word processor allows you to use the word processor with which you feel most comfortable.

CREATING TEXT FOR VENTURA

Because you will be using your word processor to create text especially for use with Ventura, you should first consider the capabilities of each. For example, you should use Ventura for formatting. (Formatting includes setting margins, tabs, and line spacing.) The basic format of your documents created in your word processor is not important. Ventura will take care of the formatting for you. Use the following guidelines when you create text for Ventura:

1. Ventura has powerful formatting capabilities; therefore, you should not insert tabs, special margins, or line-spacing commands in your word processor text.

2. Do not insert spaces in the first line of each paragraph. Instead, use Ventura's Indent feature to adjust the indent space.

3. Do not place two spaces in your text to separate the punctuation of one sentence and the uppercase letter of the next sentence unless you prefer the extra space. Although in typing you are trained to insert this extra space after a period, colon, question mark, or exclamation mark, you should not do so in text files that will be imported into Ventura unless you want extra white space in your text.

4. Do not center text in your word processor; you will only add extra spaces that will confuse Ventura. Remember, even though you cannot see a space on your computer screen, to a word processing program or to Ventura, the space is a character. Ventura sees the space as a character and adjusts the text just as if there was some other character in the same position. Extra spaces will usually cause problems that you can avoid by simply not inserting them in word processor text.

5. Use a ragged right margin in your word processing text files. Do not right-justify text.

6. Use the word processor's spelling checker before you load text files into Ventura. Special codes and words will be entered into the text by Ventura, and your word processor's spell checker will not recognize those commands.

7. Do not use the word processor to underline, bold, or italicize an entire paragraph. Instead, rely on Ventura to change the text attribute. You can use the word processor to emphasize a single word or phrase within a paragraph.

8. Enter special text attributes (discussed later) to save time and eliminate errors.

9. Do not enter two returns between paragraphs. Enter only one return to separate paragraphs.

If you find it too difficult to break some of your old typing and word processing preparation habits, you can use the search and replace feature of your word processor to adjust text files to Ventura requirements. For example, you could place a command in your search and replace function to locate all .(Space)(Space) entries and replace them with .(Space). Or you could search and replace for two returns (if you normally place two in your text files to separate paragraphs) and replace them with one return. Use all the powerful features of your word processor to edit your text as thoroughly as possible before importing it into Ventura.

Tabs

With a word processor, tabs are frequently used to indent paragraphs and create tables. As already stated, you should no longer use tabs to insert indents into your paragraphs. Instead, you should use Ventura's In/Outdent feature in the Alignment option of the Paragraph menu heading.

If you use tabs in word processing text files, you are asking for problems when you import the text into Ventura. When you press the Tab key while creating a word processing file, some word processors insert a predetermined amount of space, and others insert the ASCII code (^I) for tabs. Ventura will only recognize ^I as a tab. Another tab alignment problem occurs if you use justified text in your word processing files because the tab settings in Ventura differ from the tab settings in your word processor text file, which usually results in misalignment. Review Chapter 12 for more information about tabs and tables, but generally avoid tabs in your regular text files.

Proofreading

No matter how good you are with your word processor, no matter how great a typist you are, and no matter how many text editing and checking programs you use, enough cannot be said about the value of old-fashioned proofreading. High-tech writing aids leave much to be desired when it comes to proofreading. Consider, for a moment, the following headline:

GIANT LIZARD PARALYZES CITY

Nothing is wrong with that headline. It attracts attention, contains no misspelled words, and is grammatically correct. The only problem is that the headline was supposed to read as follows:

GIANT BLIZZARD PARALYZES CITY

A computer spell checking program would not have caught such a contextual error. Proofreading now prevents embarrassment later.

IMPORTING WORD PROCESSING FILES

Ventura can read text files created with the IBM DisplayWrite 3 and 4, Microsoft Word/Windows Write, Ashton-Tate's MultiMate, WordPerfect, WordStar, Xerox Writer, or XyWrite word processors. Ventura can also import and accept any ASCII text file. Because virtually every word processing program can produce ASCII text, you can use almost any other word processor with Ventura as well.

The following file name extensions are frequently used in naming word processing files:

ASCII	.TXT
DisplayWrite	.DCA
MS Word	.DOC
MultiMate	.DOC
WordPerfect	.WP
WordStar	.WS
Xerox Writer	.XWP
XyWrite	.TXT

PREFORMATTING TEXT FILES

Ventura does not require that you preformat a text file. When you preformat a text file, you enter codes that will automatically produce specific formats when that text file is loaded into Ventura. You can format all text files directly in Ventura, but when combined with your word processing macro or a product like SuperKey, you will find that preformatting text files may be the fastest and easiest way to work with Ventura. This strategy is especially useful if you will be publishing long documents or documents built using the contents of a database.

To understand how preformatting files can save you time and work, consider how Ventura operates. First, you create a text file on your favorite word processor. When it is ready to be imported into Ventura, you start Ventura and select your style sheet; then, you load the text with the proper format. You may make a few minor adjustments and then assign tags to the various paragraphs. You must also give the file a Ventura chapter name. Then, when you save your file, Ventura saves the chapter as well as your text file, but Ventura has inserted its own codes and tags into the text file.

It is easy to grasp how preformatting a text file works: you simply place the information about the format (e.g., paragraph tags or text attributes) into the file before loading it into Ventura. If the text document is preformatted, all you need to work on in Ventura is the actual layout or paste-up phase of preparing your document for final output.

You can preformat the following items before importing text into Ventura:

- Text attributes, such as bold or italics
- Special characters
- Formatting information
- Footnotes and indexes
- Tag names

Entering Text Attributes

Text attributes are activated in Ventura when the program encounters a code letter inserted between two angle brackets (< >). For example, if Ventura finds <U> embedded in the text, it underlines that text. A <B> code begins bold, and <I> activates italicized type. When Ventura locates angle brackets in a text file, it does not print the brackets, nor does it display on the screen the brackets or the code within the brackets. It simply recognizes the brackets as a code for its formats. Text attribute codes can be placed anywhere in a document as long as they are always surrounded by the brackets.

> **Tip**: If you must actually use angle brackets in your text, you must use double angle brackets to make them appear on the screen and print. For example, if you wanted to print <DOGS>, you would enter the text as <<DOGS>>.

You can insert many different text attribute codes in a text file, including the following, where *nnn* = the numerical value you want:

Base line jump	<J*nnn*>
Begin kerning	<K*nnn*>
Bold-weight type	<B>
Color index	<C*nnn*>
Double underline	<=>
Italic type	<I>
Light-weight type	<L>
Medium-weight type	<M>
Overscore	<O>
Point size	<P*nnn*>
Resume normal	<D>
Small	<S>
Strike-through	<X>
Subscript	<V>
Superscript	<^>
Typeface	<F*nnn*>
Underline	<U>

You can insert the following spacing codes in your text.

<table>
<tr><td>Discretionary hyphen</td><td><-></td></tr>
<tr><td>Em Space</td><td><_></td></tr>
<tr><td>En Space</td><td><~></td></tr>
<tr><td>Figure Space</td><td><+></td></tr>
<tr><td>Line Break</td><td><R></td></tr>
<tr><td>Non-breaking space</td><td><N></td></tr>
<tr><td>Thin space</td><td><|></td></tr>
</table>

Color can be assigned to text. Code numbers for colors are as follows:

White	0
Black	1
Red	2
Green	3
Blue	4
Cyan	5
Yellow	6
Magenta	7
Reset to Tag Color	255

Typefaces can also be specified in text files. The availability of typefaces depends on the installation procedure and the available fonts. Following are examples of possible font codes:

Courier	1
Swiss (Helvetica)	2
Dutch (Times Roman)	14
Prestige Elite	103

You can determine codes for specific fonts by referring to Appendix K in the Ventura reference guide. A complete listing of typefaces with their identification numbers is also available in that guide.

In addition, there are codes for specifying footnote text, picture frame anchor text, and index text. These codes are as follows:

Footnote	<$Ffootnote text>
Index (primary and secondary reference)	<$Iprimary;secondary>
Index ("See" references)	<$Sprimary;secondary>
Index ("See also" references)	<$Aprimary;secondary>
Picture Frame anchor same page	<$&anchor name>
Picture Frame anchor below	<$&anchor name[v]>
Picture Frame anchor above	<$&anchor name[^]>

Many word processors also include a feature that allows you to insert **hidden text** (i.e., text for notes or comments that you want to see on the screen but that you do not want to print). This code works the same way in Ventura. You can use the following code in your word processor text files to create hidden text in Ventura:

<$!hidden text>

You must then resume normal text or turn off the special format you have inserted. The code to resume normal text is <D>. Insert <D> in the text at the point where you want to stop producing the added format.

Following are examples of how these text attributes can be added in your word processor text files and how the resume normal text code should be inserted:

To create an italicized word, enter

<I>Dog<D>

To create a bold, italicized word, enter

<BI>Dog<D>

To create a bold, italicized word in the color green, enter

<BIC3>Dog<D>

You need not insert <D> if the final word or words in a paragraph include a special text attribute. In Ventura, the text will automatically revert back to normal at the end of a paragraph.

New Attributes vs. Old Attributes

If you enter new attributes, previously entered attributes are terminated. For example, if you first bold the text and then add the italics code, the bold text will stop without the insertion of the resume normal text code. Consider the following examples:

If you enter

The dog is <B>big and <I>old.

the result is as follows:

The dog is **big and** *old.*

To have the word "old" both italicized and bolded, you must enter the following:

The dog is <B>big and <BI>old.

Word Processing Magic with Ventura

If you are using Microsoft Word or Windows Write, MultiMate, WordPerfect, WordStar, Xerox Writer, or XyWrite, Ventura automatically converts some of your word processor's text attribute codes. For example, if you are using WordPerfect and press the F6 key to make a word bold, WordPerfect inserts a bold code into its text. When the text is imported into Ventura, WordPerfect's bold code will automatically be converted into Ventura's bold code.

For example, WordPerfect's code for bold type is as follows:

[B]dog[b]

In this example, the word "dog" would be bold. If you were importing WordPerfect text into Ventura, you could format the text to be made bold with Ventura's bold code,

<B>dog<D>

or with WordPerfect's bold code,

[B]dog[b]

Ventura automatically translates the following word processor formatting codes:

- Begin and End Bold
- Begin and End Superscript
- Begin and End Subscript
- Begin and End Strike-through
- Underline
- Discretionary Hyphen
- Non-break Space

The Problem with Italics

When manuscripts are prepared, the writer usually underlines a word for emphasis. In most published works, such words are usually italicized when typeset.

You can use three different approaches to this problem.

- You could have your authors continue to work as always, and when the text is imported into Ventura, you could look for the underlined words and convert them to italics.

- Alternatively, you could use the word processor to search for the underline codes and replace them with the <I> italics code. You would also need to insert the resume normal text code <D> in the text following the word or phrase to be italicized.

- The other solution is to have the manuscript's author insert the codes <I> and <D> around words to be italicized.

Non-Break Spaces

This feature of your word processor is called by various names: hard space, required space, non-break space, etc. The non-break feature allows you to keep together words that should always appear together (e.g., so they won't be separated at the end of a line). The non-break space is particularly useful for names, dates, measurements, and initials. For example, "July 19, 1942," "12.4 gals.," and "DisplayWrite 4" should each contain non-break spaces between all words and numbers. Entering <N> in your word processor text will produce a non-break space in Ventura. When running Ventura, you can insert non-break spaces by pressing the Ctrl/Space Bar key combination.

Entering Special Characters

Ventura includes a set of characters for many foreign language applications and a symbol character set for some mathematical formulas. If you have installed PostScript fonts, you can also use special symbols from symbol sets. One such set is called Dingbats. To insert one of these special symbols, just enclose in brackets the number of the character you want to use.

For example, the code number for the symbol used to signify a copyright is 189. To obtain the copyright symbol (©), just insert <189> in your text at the exact place where you want the copyright symbol to appear.

A complete list of special characters and their number codes is displayed in Appendix E of the Ventura reference guide. Also see Figure 3.1.

Deci-mal	Char Set 1	Char Set 2
1-31	not used	
32	space	space
33	!	!
34	"	∀
35	#	#
36	$	∃
37	%	%
38	&	&
39	'	∍
40	(	(
41	)	)
42	*	*
43	+	+
44	,	,
45	-	−
46	.	.
47	/	/
48	0	0
49	1	1
50	2	2
51	3	3
52	4	4
53	5	5
54	6	6
55	7	7
56	8	8
57	9	9
58	:	:
59	;	;
60	<	<
61	=	=
62	>	>

Deci-mal	Char Set 1	Char Set 2
63	?	?
64	@	≅
65	A	Α
66	B	Β
67	C	Χ
68	D	Δ
69	E	Ε
70	F	Φ
71	G	Γ
72	H	Η
73	I	Ι
74	J	ϑ
75	K	Κ
76	L	Λ
77	M	Μ
78	N	Ν
79	O	Ο
80	P	Π
81	Q	Θ
82	R	Ρ
83	S	Σ
84	T	Τ
85	U	Υ
86	V	ς
87	W	Ω
88	X	Ξ
89	Y	Ψ
90	Z	Ζ
91	[	[
92	\	∴
93	]	]
94	^	⊥

Deci-mal	Char Set 1	Char Set 2
95	_	_
96	‘	‾
97	a	α
98	b	β
99	c	χ
100	d	δ
101	e	ε
102	f	φ
103	g	γ
104	h	η
105	i	ι
106	j	φ
107	k	κ
108	l	λ
109	m	μ
110	n	ν
111	o	ο
112	p	π
113	q	θ
114	r	ρ
115	s	σ
116	t	τ
117	u	υ
118	v	ϖ
119	w	ω
120	x	ξ
121	y	ψ
122	z	ζ
123	{	{
124	|	|
125	}	}
126	~	~

A style sheet called CHARSET.STY was supplied with your copy of Ventura Publisher. You should print this style sheet to create a chart of the various symbols available.

Figure 3.1

Decimal	Char Set 1	Char Set 2
127		
128	Ç	
129	ü	
130	é	′
131	â	≤
132	ä	/
133	à	∞
134	å	ƒ
135	ç	♣
136	ê	♦
137	ë	♥
138	è	♠
139	ï	↔
140	î	←
141	ì	↑
142	Ä	→
143	Å	↓
144	É	°
145	æ	±
146	Æ	″
147	ô	≥
148	ö	×
149	ò	∝
150	û	∂
151	ù	•
152	ÿ	÷
153	Ö	≠
154	Ü	≡
155	¢	≈
156	£	…
157	¥	|
158	¤	—

Decimal	Char Set 1	Char Set 2
159	ƒ	↵
160	á	ℵ
161	í	
162	ó	
163	ú	℘
164	ñ	⊗
165	Ñ	⊕
166	ª	∅
167	º	∩
168	¿	∪
169	“	⊃
170	”	⊇
171	‹	⊄
172	›	⊂
173	¡	⊆
174	«	∈
175	»	∉
176	ã	∠
177	õ	∇
178	Ø	®
179	ø	©
180	œ	™
181	Œ	Π
182	À	√
183	Ã	·
184	Õ	¬
185	§	∧
186	‡	∨
187	†	⇔
188	¶	⇐
189	©	⇑
190	®	⇒

Decimal	Char Set 1	Char Set 2
191	™	⇓
192	„	◊
193	…	〈
194	‰	®
195	•	©
196	–	™
197	—	Σ
198	°	⎛
199	Á	⎜
200	Â	⎝
201	È	⎡
202	Ê	⎢
203	Ë	⎣
204	Ì	⎧
205	Í	⎨
206	Î	⎩
207	Ï	⎪
208	Ò	
209	Ó	〉
210	Ô	∫
211	Š	⌠
212	š	⎮
213	Ù	⌡
214	Ú	⎞
215	Û	⎟
216	Ÿ	⎠
217	ß	⎤
218		
219		
220		
221		
222		

Figure 3.1 (continued)

Entering Formatting Information

Formatting information that changes the typeface or type size of particular text can also be inserted by using angle brackets. The code <F*nnn*>, where *nnn* is the code for the particular font or typefce, allows you to choose typefaces available in your font library.

The code <P*nnn*> permits you to choose the point size of your font. You can add this formatting information just as you would add any other special format codes in a word processor text file.

Entering Footnotes and Indexes

Text for footnotes and indexes can be created in your word processor rather than in Ventura.

For footnote text, enter <$F>, including the text of the footnote between the angle brackets. A typical footnote entry might resemble the following:

<$FRefer to 1987 Annual Report for more information.>

The bracket codes for setting up indexes are a bit more complex because Ventura offers different levels of indexing. Consider the following example index entry:

Printers
  AST
  Hewlett-Packard
  PostScript
  See also Installation

In this example, the "Printers" entry is a first level or **primary** entry. The names of the printers—AST, Hewlett-Packard, and Postscript—are the **secondary** entries.

The angle bracket code for index is <$I>. The <$I> is followed by the primary reference. Any secondary references are preceded by a semicolon. For example, the index code for the "AST" entry in the previous example would be the following:

<$IPrinters;AST>

Note that there are no spaces within the angle brackets.

Ventura's indexing feature also permits the use of "See" or "See also" references. The bracket code for "See" is <$S>. The bracket code for "See also" is <$A>. To make the "See also" listing in the previous example, you would enter the following:

<$APrinters;Installation>

Ventura can also handle words that must be listed out of alphabetical order, which often happens with titles that contain the word "The." If you were indexing "The First Street Warehouse," you would want the listing under "First Street Warehouse," not under "The." To handle this special situation, you would enter the following:

<$IThe First Street Warehouse[First Street Warehouse]>

Entering Tag Names

Paragraph tags in Ventura are special formatting codes that affect entire paragraphs or any information between two paragraph returns. If you know the names of the paragraph tags you will be using with Ventura-formatted text, you can insert the names of the paragraph tags as you prepare the text file in your word processor.

The advantage of adding these tags in the text file is that when you import your text file into Ventura, the document will be automatically formatted as specified in the Ventura style sheet you use. (See Chapter 8 for information on creating Ventura paragraph tags and style sheets.) You will eliminate or at least reduce the need to use the paragraph-tagging function within Ventura because you will have already assigned your tags.

Ventura's preformatting code for paragraph tags is the at sign (@) followed by an equal sign (=). In the far left margin of your word processor paragraph, type @. Then, without adding a space, type the name of the paragraph tag. Add a space, an equal sign (=), and another space; then, type the text. For example, if your headline is GIANT BLIZZARD PARALYZES CITY, the entry would resemble the following:

@HEADING = GIANT BLIZZARD PARALYZES CITY

Whenever a paragraph tag is inserted into a text file, Ventura uses the attributes assigned to that paragraph tag in the style sheet until it encounters a hard return, which indicates the end of a paragraph. Ventura then reverts to normal text.

If text is not assigned a specific tag, Ventura applies text attributes assigned to Body Text, which is Ventura's standard, or default, paragraph tag for any document. Accordingly, you need not enter a paragraph tag for Body Text.

If you have three paragraphs in a row with the same tag name, and the text is not body text, you must enter the name of the text on the first line of each paragraph. As stated previously, paragraph tag names do not carry over onto the next paragraph. The hard return, which identifies the end of a paragraph, turns off the paragraph tag.

Capitalization in the paragraph tag name does not matter, but when preformatting, you must spell the paragraph tag name exactly as it appears in the style sheet. The paragraph tags "Subheading" and "Subheadings" are not the same to Ventura. If Ventura cannot match a paragraph tag in your text with one in the selected style sheet, it will apply the Body Text tag attributes to the paragraph with the unidentified paragraph tag.

Parafilter

You should not enter double returns between paragraphs in Ventura unless you want extra white space. For each return, Ventura inserts a predetermined amount of spacing. Even if there is no text between returns, Ventura will still treat each return as a paragraph.

However, if you don't use double returns, your text will be very difficult to read while you work with it in its original word processing format. The answer to this formatting problem is to use Ventura's Parafilter command when preformatting your text files. You can insert double returns in your text so you can see your paragraphs, and by placing the Parafilter command at the left margin on the very first line of your text, you can instruct Ventura to ignore the second return.

The Parafilter command is as follows:

@PARAFILTER ON =

You should be aware that if you use the parafilter command, once the text file has been loaded into Ventura and then saved, the double returns will be eliminated because Ventura strips them out of your text, but the Parafilter command does make your word processing text easier to read during preparation.

Working with ASCII Files

Most word processing programs—as well as other popular database programs, spreadsheets, and notepad programs—can generate ASCII text. The difference between ASCII text and a word processing text file, as far as Ventura is concerned, is the use of soft and hard returns. In an ASCII text file, a hard return is placed at the end of each line of text. In contrast, in a word processing file, a soft return is placed at the end of each line. In an ASCII text file, two hard returns are inserted to indicate the end of a paragraph. In a word processing text program, only one hard return is used to indicate the end of the paragraph.

When you import an ASCII text file into Ventura, a single hard return is translated into a soft return. When Ventura encounters two returns in an ASCII text file, one hard return is maintained, and the second one is deleted.

In an ASCII text file, you must use angle brackets to identify special text attributes, such as bold <B> or underline <U>.

Many popular programs, such as dBASE III, Lotus 1-2-3, and SideKick, produce ASCII text files. As long as you know how to generate ASCII text from these other programs, data from these program files can be imported into Ventura. Remember to use the .TXT extension with an ASCII text file.

MORE TIPS FOR PREFORMATTING TEXT

All this work to enter formats in text with your word processor may seem to be just that—work. You may wonder if you can do the work faster in Ventura.

At first, you may spend time creating formats in Ventura, but as you become more familiar with using your word processor to make text for use especially in Ventura, you will find that it makes for faster production to place these codes directly into word processor text.

Following are hints for more easily inserting Ventura format codes directly into your word processor text files.

1. Use macros for format commands. Use either the macro command in your word processor or an add-on program, such as SuperKey. Then, you can insert Ventura format codes easily and quickly with just a keystroke or two.

2. Review Ventura text files after they have been formatted in Ventura by reloading them into your word processor to see how Ventura has added the codes into your document. All you must do is learn how to duplicate those codes in your word processor to save time in Ventura.

3. Use your word processor's search-and-replace feature to help solve special problems, such as two spaces inserted after periods. You can simply replace all double spaces with a single space.

Finally, you may decide never to use preformatted text files. You can always perform all formatting work in Ventura; however, to save time and make Ventura easier to use, it is recommended that you implement a system of preformatting text files in your word processor.

HELP WITH YOUR WRITING

In addition to the programs RightWriter and Grammatik II mentioned in Chapter 2, some other programs that might help you get started or improve your writing are Headliner and Off The Wall, both from the Salinon Corporation. These programs are designed to help you start the writing process. Headliner generates expressions and phrases that can be used as promotional expressions. Off The Wall creates funny, silly, or just plain fun expressions. Both can help you formulate ideas and just might generate the phrase you need most. They are also easy to use. If you need help getting started, do not overlook these programs.

Once you have written the text, it is time to check your grammar and make improvements. While only the writer can provide final proofing, you can get help from RightWriter and Grammatik II. Both are excellent programs. They work well and with decent speed. They will help improve your writing by finding cliches, redundant expressions, and vague words. These programs also search your text for long sentences, missing punctuation, and misplaced capitalization. RightWriter and Grammatik II are well worth their cost, so do not be surprised if you use these programs as much as you use your word processor.

CHAPTER 4

GRAPHICS

Version 1.1 of Ventura Publisher offers an elementary graphics option that is probably the weakest part of the entire program; it lacks many features of today's sophisticated graphics programs.

Although Ventura graphics are limited, they can be useful. For simple graphics — a line here, a circle there, a box in the corner — Ventura's graphics will do the job.

In Ventura, however, you can't paint and draw — at least not as in other available programs. You can, however, easily add a graphics program to your toolkit. Then, just as you import text created with your word processor, you can import graphics created in your paint-and-draw programs into Ventura.

VENTURA'S GRAPHIC FUNCTION

The fourth option in the function selection box above the side bar is the Graphic Drawing function. Ventura allows you to draw lines, ellipses, rectangles, and round-edged rectangles. Any of these shapes can be filled with different shades and colors. You can also place text in a graphic box and then move the box anywhere on the page.

Before you can draw a graphic in Ventura, you must select a frame. The frame can be the underlying page frame or a frame positioned on top of the underlying page frame. To select a frame, activate Ventura's Frame function in the function selection box. If black buttons do not appear around the edge of the underlying page frame, click the mouse once inside the page's outline. To select a frame you have created, click the mouse once inside that frame.

Paint-and-Draw Programs

Many good paint-and-draw programs are available. When choosing a paint-and-draw program, base your decision on the following two criteria: files created by paint-and-draw programs must be capable of being imported into Ventura, and the paint-and-draw program must be comfortable for you to use.

Following is list of paint-and-draw programs worthy of consideration:

- Publisher's Paintbrush and PC Paintbrush
- Dr. Halo III
- HALO DPE
- GEM Draw Plus
- Microsoft Windows

Each of these programs provides good paint-and-draw capabilities. Xerox just released a utility program to allow Windows to be used with Ventura.

If you plan to use a scanner, consider adding a paint-and-draw program that can accept and edit scanned images.

Business Graphics and Charts

Lotus 1-2-3 introduced the benefits of business graphics and charts created using spreadsheet data.

Lotus graphics are easily imported into Ventura. After creating the spreadsheet (see Figure 4.1) and graph (see Figure 4.2), save the graph. Lotus 1-2-3 will save the graph in a .PIC file. Import the .PIC file into Ventura through the Load menu.

Market	March	April	May
Harrisburg PA	$12,124.00	$22,870.00	$38,674.00
Atlanta GA	$5,434.00	$13,190.00	$34,234.00
Weatherford TX	$2,311.00	$7,609.00	$21,234.00
Las Vegas NV	$9,099.00	$11,108.00	$23,450.00
TOTAL	$28,968.00	$54,777.00	$117,592.00

This figure shows a printout of a simple Lotus 1-2-3 spreadsheet. (See the entire example report in Appendix B.) After the spreadsheet was prepared, a Lotus graph (see Figure 4.2) was created.

Figure 4.1

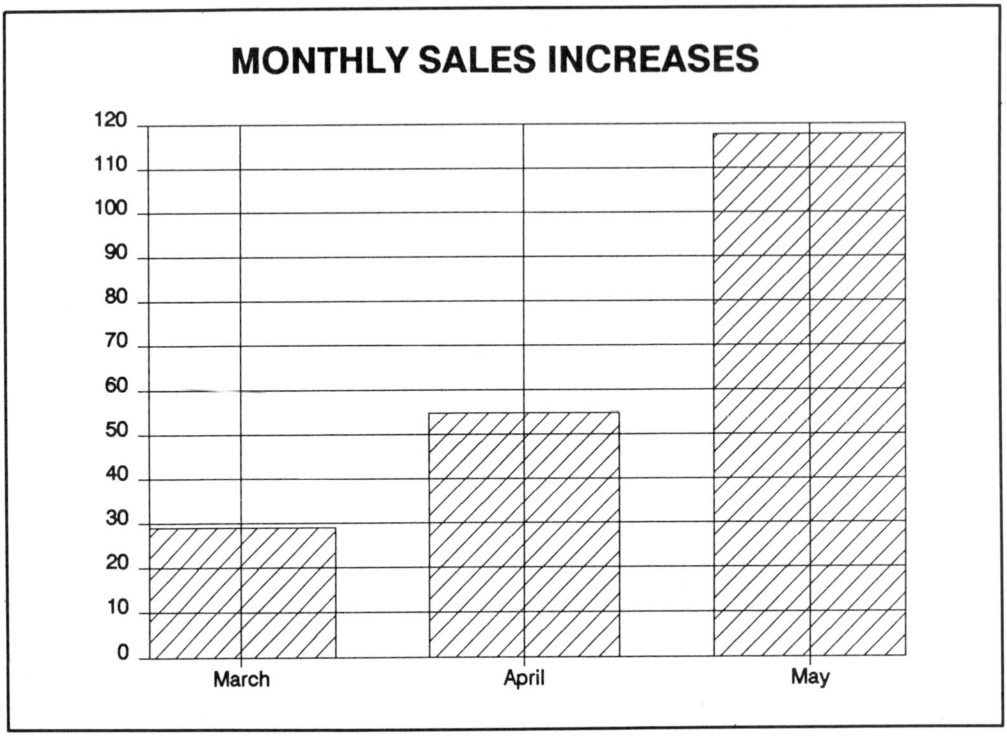

Here, a Lotus Graph was created from the data in the spreadsheet in Figure 4.1. Lotus graphs are easily imported into Ventura. Graphs help clarify text and add impact to documents.

Figure 4.2

GEM Presentation Team

The GEM Presentation Team offers extensive business graphics capabilities. GEM Graph and GEM Draw Business Library are excellent programs that can create impressive business graphs.

The GEM Presentation Team is a rather extensive package that will take some time to learn. You may, however, learn to use it more quickly than you expect because the programs look and act like Ventura. The familiar pull-down menus are quickly mastered.

Energraphics

This is a powerful program that can enhance your desktop publishing skills. Figure 4.3 illustrates an Energraphics three-dimensional graphic.

If you want your charts to have impact, this is the program to use. It offers many features and, surprisingly, is easy to learn and to use.

Energraphics creates .IMG files, which can be imported into Ventura as easily as any other file. If you need dynamic charts and drawings, you need Energraphics.

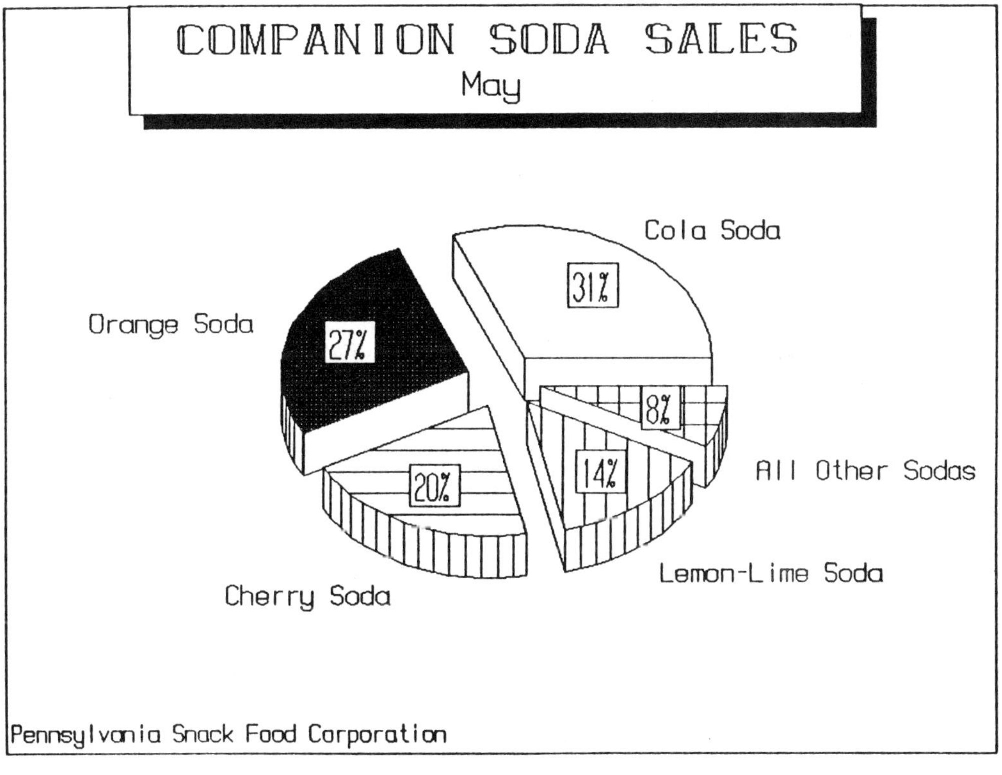

This figure shows a three-dimensional graph created using Energraphics 2.0. This graphic was also included in the final version of the example report in Appendix B.

Figure 4.3

Freelance Plus

A product from Lotus—Freelance Plus—enables you to create more stunning graphics than those created with the graph feature of Lotus 1-2-3. To import a Freelance Plus graphic, use the CGM (Computer Graphics Metafile) selection. Then, import the Freelance Plus graphic through Ventura's Load Text/Picture option under the File menu heading.

Screen-Capture Software

Depending on the documents you are producing, you may need to capture screen images. The best screen-shooting product is HOTSHOT from Symsoft. Most screen shots (pictures of computer screens) are created with this product. More importantly, not only can you snap pictures of your screens and send them directly to the laser printer, but you can also create a file and import that file directly into Ventura through the Load menu. If you find yourself needing screen shots (to illustrate a computer program, for example), HOTSHOT can do the job well. This product has also been greatly improved, and you can capture both text and graphic screens.

Another product that can capture your screens is the Freize function found in Z-Soft's Publisher's Paintbrush and PC PaintBrush programs. Freize can capture the entire screen or only a portion of the screen. Freize is simple to operate and is an added bonus when you buy Z-Soft's Publisher's Paintbrush and PC Paintbrush.

Borland's SideKick also offers a screen-capture option that can be used for text screens.

If you are using GEM's presentation team, you can use GEM's SnapShot to create screen shots.

After capturing your screens and saving them in a file, it is best to "warm boot" your computer (press the Ctrl/Alt/Delete key combination) before starting work in Ventura. Screen-capture programs take over part of RAM, which slows Ventura operation.

Clip Art

In a conventional print shop, where type and pictures are physically pasted on boards, many printers use large clip-art books that contain many different types of illustrations.

Desktop publishers can use electronic clip art. Such pictures are contained on a disk and are easily imported into Ventura (see Figure 4.4). Import the drawing as you would any other image. Select a frame, and choose the art. Then, import the art file. It is a simple process, and—unless you are an artist or have one working for you—it is one way to access professionally prepared line art.

As always, do not overdo it when it comes to clip art. A few pieces of clip art can enhance the appearance of your document; excessive clip art can make it look jammed and sloppy.

You can also use clip art with your paint programs. You can edit a picture with the airbrush and fill it with solids or patterns. You can erase portions of an image and reverse or rotate line art. You can modify drawings by adding to them, and you can combine two or more pictures. (You cannot include two or more pictures in a single frame in Ventura. You must first combine art in your paint and draw program and import the new, combined art file into Ventura.) Of course, make backup copies of your master diskettes before you begin editing the original pictures.

(See Figure 4.4 on next page)

Examples of clip art from Desktop Art by Dynamic Graphics.

Figure 4.4

Publisher's PicturePak

Publisher's PicturePak, from Marketing Graphics Incorporated, is one such electronic clip art program. Three different sets of line art are available as part of the Eye Openers series. Each program offers excellent clip art that can enhance your documents (see Figures 4.5-4.7).

This figure shows examples of clip art from Publisher's PicturePak by Marketing Graphics Incorporated.

Figure 4.5

An example of a clip art image from Publisher's PicturePak.

Figure 4.6

This example is a reduction of the same image shown in Figure 4.6. It was imported into a Ventura frame, and then the size of the frame was reduced. Clip art can be sized in Ventura by simply adjusting the frame size.

Figure 4.7

Windows Draw

The Windows Draw program from Micrografx also includes a large bundle of professional clip art. This clip art must be used in the Windows environment. Xerox has released a utility that allows Windows pictures to be used with Ventura.

Desktop Art

From Dynamic Graphics, Inc., Desktop Art is another series of electronic clip art that can easily be imported in Ventura or into a paint and draw program. Several different versions of Desktop Art are available. Each package is based on a theme such as sports, business, education, four seasons, or graphics and symbols. (See Figure 4.4.)

Desktop Art is stored in PC Paintbrush format.

More Examples of Clip Art

The addition of clip art can change the tone of your text. In this example, the bold type seems friendlier with the addition of the billboard background. This example was prepared by importing the Publisher's PicturePak clip art into a Ventura frame and positioning another frame on top of it. The text was imported on the top frame.

Figure 4.8

This clip art example shows a computer at its regular size.

Figure 4.9

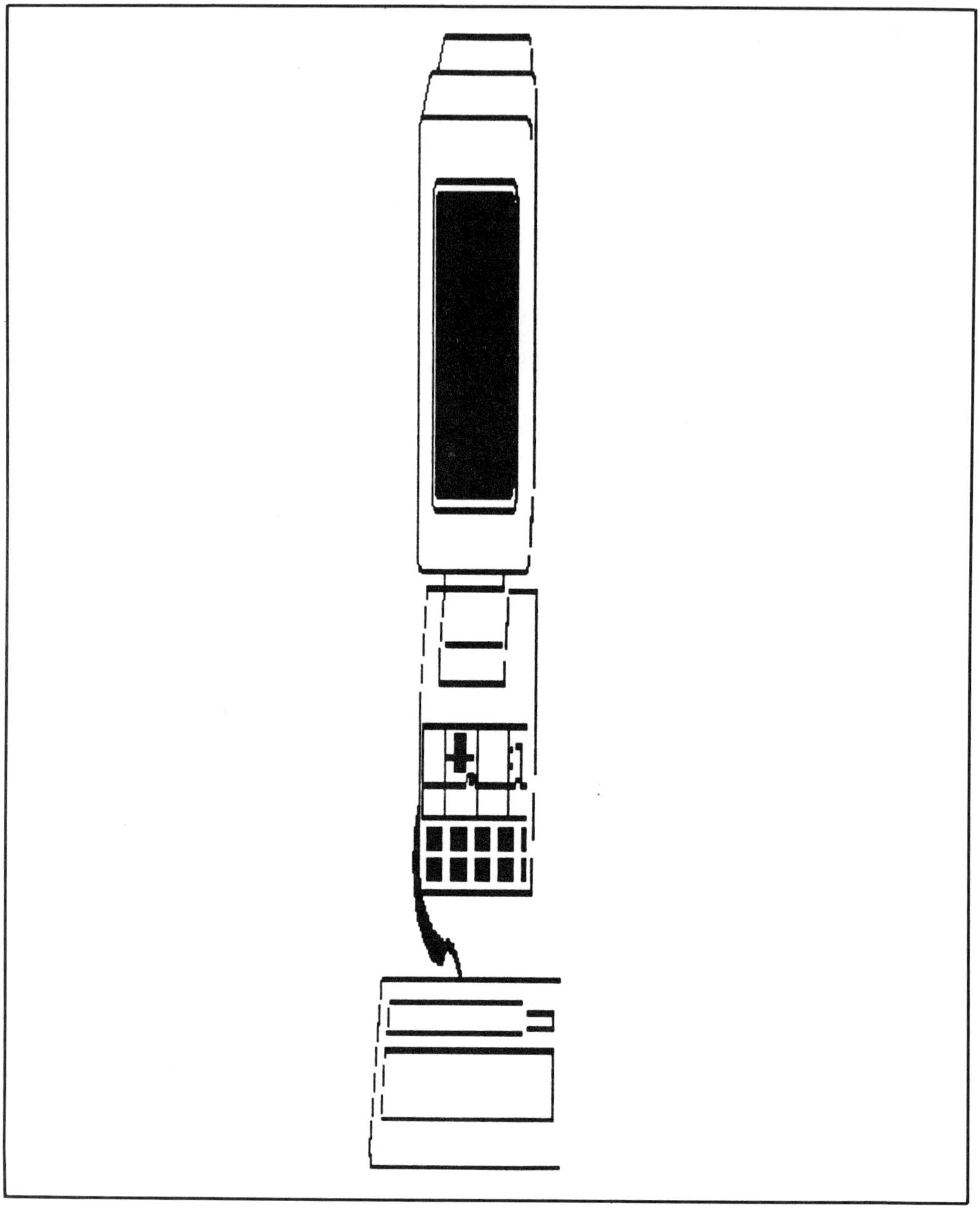

Here, the drawing shown in Figure 4.9 is stretched far out of shape. When using clip art in Ventura, you must be careful not to stretch clip art to the point of distortion.

Figure 4.10

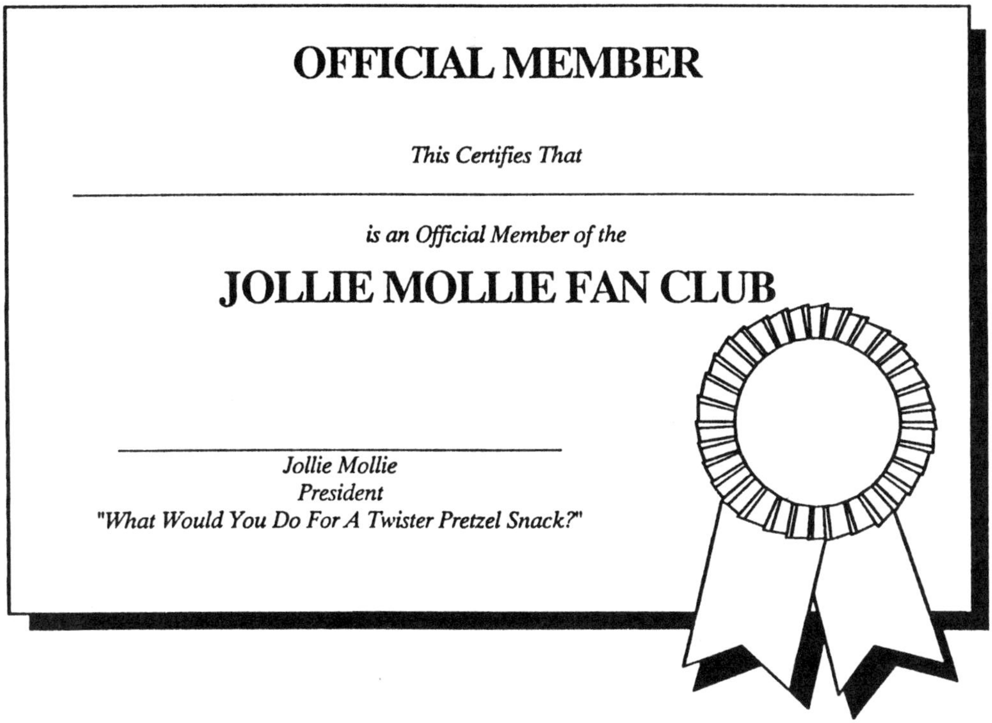

This figure shows an example of how clip art can be integrated with text. This clip art from Publisher's PicturePak was imported into Ventura, and then the text was added.

Figure 4.11

Here is an example of how clip art can enhance your documents. A piece of Publisher's PicturePak clip art was chosen to enhance the cover of a report.

Figure 4.12

IMPORTING GRAPHICS

You can import into Ventura graphics created in GEM, Lotus PIC, AutoCAD SLD, VideoShow, Encapsulated PostScript, HPGL, Computer Graphics Metafile (CGM), and MacDraw PICT. TIFF formatted files should soon be compatible with Ventura.

Working with graphics—scanned images, clip art, paint-and-draw images—takes time and patience. You must experiment with various drawings and software packages before you can achieve the results you want.

Ventura converts graphic files into its own file format. Ventura does not change the original file format, but you must have enough disk space available to fit the graphic in the original file format and the Ventura file format. GEM and HALO DPE formats are accepted by Ventura without creating an additional file, which saves disk space.

Macintosh images can be imported into Ventura, but you will need a transfer system. You must transfer the file from the Macintosh-format disk to a PC-format disk. Centram Systems' TOPS or DataViz's MacLink can transfer such files.

CHAPTER 5

SCANNERS

Scanning technology is exciting—especially to desktop publishers. A scanner works much like a photocopier: a two- or even three-dimensional object is photographed, and the information is processed into a digital format that can be recognized by a computer.

TYPES OF SCANNERS

There are two forms of scanners: optical and video. **Optical scanners** resemble and operate like photocopying machines. A bright light scans and records the image. The device that creates bit maps of scanned images is called a **Charge-Coupled Device** (CCD).

Optical scanners come in two styles. With some optical scanners, you feed the page to be scanned into the scanner. These scanners are referred to as **sheet-fed** scanners. In other models, the paper is positioned on a curved or flat bed as on a photocopying machine. These scanners are referred to as **flat-bed** scanners.

Video scanners process electronic signals generated by video cameras. More attention must be given to correct lighting when operating a video scanner. The advantage of video scanners is the ability to scan a three-dimensional object. Video scanners are discussed in more detail in Chapter 11.

HOW SCANNERS WORK

Scanners are sometimes referred to as **digitizers**. Not only can scanners digitize photographs and line art, but they can also "read" typed or printed pages. Using **Optical Character Recognition** (OCR) software, a scanner reads pages and converts typed or printed words into standard ASCII text that can then be imported into a word processor.

A scanner is hardware; to make it work, you need software. Some scanners include scanning software, but you will want to use software that is compatible with your paint-and-draw programs as well as with Ventura. Publisher's Paintbrush, Halo DPE, and the GEM Presentation Team are examples of software you can use with a scanner.

You can control the scanner within these software programs. The contrast, brightness, scanning mode, resolution, and dithering (discussed below) can be controlled. Once you have set these selections, you can scan an image. The image is then ready to load into paint-and-draw programs.

You can also crop scanned images. By cropping, you save time and disk space. You also choose between scanning a line-art or image file. You can edit, alter, or enhance the scanned image by using the various tools in your paint-and-draw program. You can then save the image into a file that Ventura will recognize.

Most scanners work in two modes: one for strictly black-and-white images and one for images with shades between blacks and whites. These shades of gray must be re-created by the laser printer, using patterns of black dots to create different shades of gray. This process of making halftones is referred to as **dithering**.

The resolution, gray scale, contrast, and brightness you choose will affect the overall quality of each image you scan.

Resolution is the number of dots per inch. Laser printers are discussed in Chapter 6. Most laser printers offer a resolution of 300 dots per inch (dpi). The more dots per inch, the higher the resolution. Photographs require many dots for adequate reproduction, while line drawings require less. If you are scanning line drawings, 75- or 100-dpi resolution will often be enough.

The **gray scale** is the amount of different available levels or shades of gray. Some scanners can only reproduce 16 shades of gray, while others—such as the DEST PC Scan-2000—can provide 256 different shades of gray. Regular line drawings require only two shades of gray: black and white. In a line drawing, pixels are either on or off; those that are on create the drawing's lines. In photographs, there are many more shades of gray. Laser printers and scanners work on a 300-dpi resolution, and it would seem this resolution could easily handle photograph reproduction—especially when you consider that newspapers and magazines often use less than 100 dpi for their photographs. The reason desktop publishing is hindered—even at 300 dpi—is because of the laser's inability to create different-sized dots. If you could originate different-sized dots with a laser printer, 300-dpi resolution would be more than sufficient.

To compensate for the single dot size, gray scales are created to mix groups of dots together (mixing white space with the black dots). The more white space, the lighter the gray. The more dots, the darker the shade of gray (see Figure 5.1).

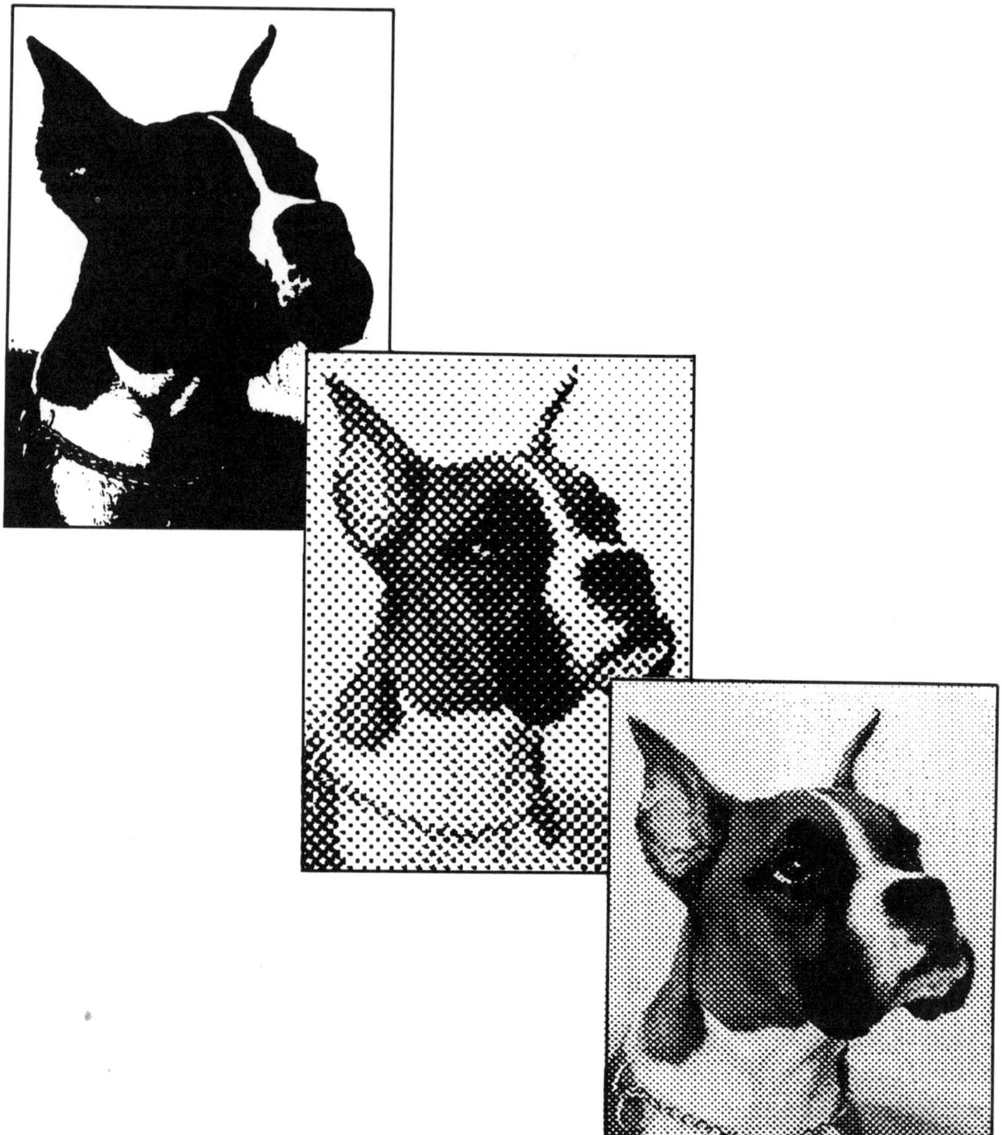

A photograph of Jollie Mollie scanned at three different gray-scale levels. The first photograph displays black and white tones only. As the gray-scale level is increased, varying dot sizes result in higher resolution.

Figure 5.1

Dithering creates halftone cells—in many cases, 16 pixels (four pixels × four pixels). Each scanned dot is then translated into a halftone cell. By using dithering in this way, you can create a gray scale, but you reduce resolution from 300 dpi to 75 dpi. It now takes 16 pixels to make a printer dot. Each of these cells looks like a tiny mosaic tile.

You must achieve a balance between multiple shades of gray and high resolution. One other important consideration in working with resolution and gray scale is the amount of necessary disk storage. A black-and-white image will not require the amount of disk storage required by a gray-scale image.

Contrast varies the intensity of the scanned images by adjusting the darkest dark section and the lightest light section. The contrast is the difference between these two levels.

Brightness controls the amount of light used to scan an image. Too much brightness uses too much light and "washes" detail out of the picture. Too little brightness (too much darkness) does not permit all the image's detail to be scanned. Obviously, the brightness must be correctly adjusted along with the contrast. Just as you adjust these controls on your television set, you must also adjust them on your scanner.

SCANNING SOFTWARE

Depending on the type of work you will be producing, you may decide not to use the scanner's software and instead use your paint-and-draw software.

Choosing a paint-and-draw program is important. Again, you want a program to create image files that are easily imported into Ventura. Publisher's Paintbrush, Halo DPE, and GEM's Paint offer excellent scanning capabilities. The image can then be touched up or edited and quickly imported into Ventura.

Dest PC-2000

Dest's PC-2000 scanner leads the pack with a 256-gray-scale level. Other scanners offer only 16 different levels of gray.

CHAPTER 6

LASER PRINTERS

THE LASER PRINTER

At COMDEX in Las Vegas, Nevada, in the fall of 1983, a company better known for cameras than computer gear made an announcement that would deliver desktop publishing to the public. At the time, little attention was paid to the Canon Corporation's announcement that it was offering other companies its laser printer engines, which, when purchased in significant quantities, would cost less than $1000.

The Canon Corporation's laser printer engines included all the mechanical parts of the printer. The electronic circuitry to control the laser printer engine was the only other requirement for putting these machines to work.

The first company to use the now available Canon Laser Printer Engine was Hewlett Packard. Hewlett-Packard designed its own controller, which was appropriately called HPPCL (Hewlett-Packard Printer Command Language). The result was the HP LaserJet, which found instant success and acceptance. Other companies followed Hewlett-Packard's leadership, such as Apple and QMS. More laser printers meant more options. Desktop publishing had arrived.

The laser printer engine is the mechanical part of the laser printer that controls the quality of the printing. The most important characteristics of a laser printer include its ability to produce shades of gray, distinct and sharp characters, graphics, and just plain old dark black text (the blacker, the better). Other important considerations are paper handling and the speed of the printing process. Compatibility with commercial typesetters is another consideration in choosing a laser printer.

The electronic circuitry, called the **controller**, determines what fonts are available for use and the capabilities of graphics reproduction. Most of the laser printer's capabilities are determined by the controller and not by the laser printer engine.

When Ricoh and Xerox laser printer engines emerged, more technology was available. The Canon laser printer engine uses a white-black technology. When printing, portions of the drum are struck by the laser and are made identical to the areas of black that will be printed on the paper. In contrast, the Xerox and Ricoh engines use the opposite approach. Areas marked on the drum of the laser printer match the unprinted, or white, areas of the page.

Laser printers are similar to photocopiers. Both laser printers and photocopiers use a bright light to transfer an image onto a print drum; however, laser printers use a light beam (the laser) to scan the image, leaving a positive electrical image on the print drum, while photocopiers use reflected light and create a negative image on the print drum.

The toner in a laser printer is attracted to the positive image. As the print drum rotates, the paper is pushed through the laser printer. It is guided through the laser printer between the print drum and a special string-like device called a transfer corona. This transfer corona does not touch the drum but transfers the image on the drum to the paper. The characters are then fused to the paper by a fixing process. The images are permanently secured onto the paper with heat or with pressure rollers.

Commercial typesetting machines offer far higher resolution than laser printers. Most notably, Allied Linotype's Linotronic 100 offers 1270-dpi (dots-per-inch) resolution, and the Linotronic 300 provides 2540-dpi resolution; however, laser printers offer many outstanding features, some of which are advantages over commercial typesetting equipment. Today's laser printers cost far less than commercial typesetters. Laser printers rival the speed of any commercial typesetter. Output from a laser printer is ready for reproduction, whereas output from a commercial typesetter is often only one step toward preparing a camera-ready, finished document. Laser printers are compatible with many different forms of personal computers and are small, efficient, and quiet. A laser printer is easy to use and can easily mix graphics and text, a task only the most expensive typesetting machines can perform.

Several types of laser print engines are used in today's laser printers. The most modern engines offer blacker blacks. Today's popular laser engines are the Canon LBP-SX (used in the Hewlett-Packard Series II Laser Printers) and the Ricoh 1060. Both are improvements upon earlier laser engines, and both offer excellent results and acceptable speed (six to eight pages per minute). Both print blacker blacks. On a photocopier, even grey blacks produced by your laser printer are reproduced as blacker blacks; however, in preparation for the printing process, the blacker the blacks your laser printer can produce, the better.

The Raster Image Processor

Perhaps better known as the controller, the **Raster Image Processor** (RIP) commands the laser printer's operation. Most controllers are located inside the laser printer, although some RIP's are located in a controller board in a slot in the computer.

The capabilities of the controller determine printer output. The controller uses software to manage its control of the printer output. This software is commonly called the **printer command language** (PCL). Ventura is compatible with virtually every printer command language available.

Although Ventura can easily work with Adobe's PostScript and Hewlett-Packard's printer command language (the two most popular printer command languages in use today), you'll soon see that Ventura's abilities change within the confines of the printer command language you are using (see Figure 6.1).

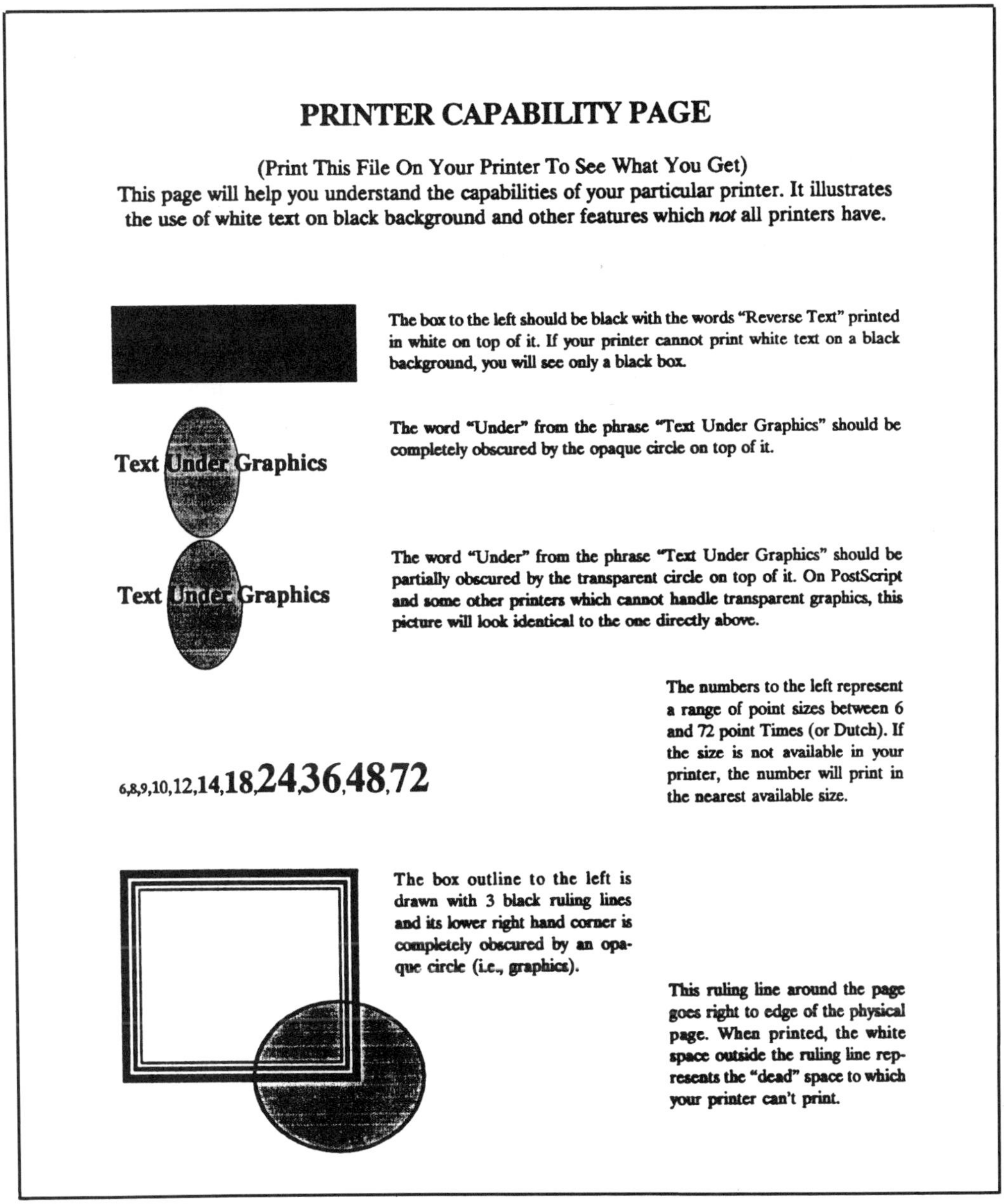

PRINTER CAPABILITY PAGE

(Print This File On Your Printer To See What You Get)

This page will help you understand the capabilities of your particular printer. It illustrates the use of white text on black background and other features which *not* all printers have.

The box to the left should be black with the words "Reverse Text" printed in white on top of it. If your printer cannot print white text on a black background, you will see only a black box.

Text Under Graphics

The word "Under" from the phrase "Text Under Graphics" should be completely obscured by the opaque circle on top of it.

Text Under Graphics

The word "Under" from the phrase "Text Under Graphics" should be partially obscured by the transparent circle on top of it. On PostScript and some other printers which cannot handle transparent graphics, this picture will look identical to the one directly above.

6,8,9,10,12,14,18,24,36,48,72

The numbers to the left represent a range of point sizes between 6 and 72 point Times (or Dutch). If the size is not available in your printer, the number will print in the nearest available size.

The box outline to the left is drawn with 3 black ruling lines and its lower right hand corner is completely obscured by an opaque circle (i.e., graphics).

This ruling line around the page goes right to edge of the physical page. When printed, the white space outside the ruling line represents the "dead" space to which your printer can't print.

To test the capability of your laser printer, load and print the chapter called CAPABILI.CHP, which was included with your copy of Ventura. The output should resemble Figure 6.1.

Figure 6.1

PostScript vs. Hewlett-Packard's Printer Command Language

PostScript is probably the most prevalent printer command language available today. After developing PostScript, Adobe Systems began licensing the use of PostScript page-description language by other companies that manufacture laser printers. Apple Computer Corporation uses PostScript in its LaserWriter, as does QMS in some of its laser printers. Most notably, Linotype's Linotronic 100 and 300 models also use the PostScript printer command language.

PostScript defines a typefont by its outline or shape, which is depicted in a computer code rather than a fixed-dot pattern. Because these outlines or shapes can be manipulated into any size, they act like graphic images. You only need one outline font and can make many different sizes from one typeface.

PostScript permits the addition of special effects (e.g., patterns, shading, deliberate stretching, tilting, spiraling, distorting, and rotation) to its type fonts.

PostScript opens the door to many different options. Unfortunately, although you can now import Encapsulated PostScript files into Ventura (using .EPS as the extension), there are not yet any Encapsulated PostScript graphics programs available for the PC/DOS and MS/DOS-based computer. There are rumors in the industry, however, that several such graphics programs are under development and will be available in the immediate future. The best alternative for creating an Encapsulated PostScript file is to use a Macintosh computer and a program like Cricket Draw or Adobe Illustrator. Then, by using a program such as PC MacBridge by Tangent Technologies or TOPS conversion program, you can import the Encapsulated PostScript program into Ventura.

As soon as Encapsulated PostScript can be generated with an IBM PC/DOS- or MS/DOS-based computer, Ventura's graphics capabilities will increase dramatically. The important point to remember is that Ventura (version 1.1) is ready to receive Encapsulated PostScript files now. Perhaps by the time you read these words, you will be able to generate Encapsulated PostScript on the same computer that runs Ventura for you.

The other major printer command language is the Hewlett-Packard (HP) PCL. The typefonts are created by a series of dot patterns. More fonts must be included on your disk to use the HP PCL. The HP PCL runs faster than PostScript; however, Ventura version 1.1 has increased the speed of PostScript by nearly 30 percent as compared to the earlier version of Ventura.

Hewlett-Packard is currently working on a second version of its PCL. The new version is supposed to make HP's PCL more versatile. If you are using an HP printer, keep watching for more information about the upgraded version of PCL.

DPI and Gray Scale

Dots-per-inch (dpi) is determined by how many dots a printer can place within a square inch. Today's laser printers are capable of producing 300 dpi. These dots form the graphics and characters in your documents.

Type produced with 300 dpi is near typeset quality; however, a close examination of such type shows ragged edges. Higher resolution is required to achieve true typeset quality. The Linotronic 100 (used by commercial typesetters) produces an output of 1270 dots per square inch and offers four times the resolution available from a laser printer while the Linotronic 300 provides eight times the resolution available from today's laser printers. Although a higher resolution is sometimes needed to make type look clean and sharp, many graphics are suitably reproduced with only 100 dpi.

Photographs create an entirely new problem. First, recall that a photograph is reproduced by printing; it is not duplicated in a photographic process with light-sensitive paper. In the printing process, the photograph must be reproduced by imprinting tiny dots of ink on the paper. Halftone screens of the original photo are used to determine where the dots should be located. A gray scale is established by varying the number of dots imprinted.

In a regular printing process, screens consisting of 120 to 150 lines are used to reproduce most of the photographs that appear in magazines or books. In newspapers, a coarser screen is used—often one consisting of only 65 to 100 lines.

Unfortunately, a laser printer can produce only one size dot. In newspapers, dot sizes vary, so a photograph in a newspaper can be reasonably reproduced with only a 65-line screen. Less resolution is required because larger dots can be used.

Paint programs and scanners produce bit maps. A **bit map** is a graphic image formed by the dots, but when imported into Ventura, it is called an **image**. The bit map determines the position of the dots and creates the shades of gray.

In a laser printer, the various shades of gray are finally determined by the capability of the software controlling the RIP.

Printer Speed

Most laser printers normally run at 9600 baud, which sounds fast, but when you consider the type of documents Ventura actually creates, it is not really that fast. Connecting your laser printer to the parallel port instead of using the serial channel speeds up printing.

Printing with a Typesetter and Proofing with a Laser Printer

Many documents you may want to publish will require higher resolution than a laser printer offers. In these cases, you can use your laser printer to make a copy of your document for proofing before sending it to a service bureau, or commercial typesetter, for more expensive output.

If you are using a PostScript laser printer and will be sending your disk files to a PostScript- driven typesetter, you need not change any settings in the Set Printer Info dialog box. The only difference between the two outputs will be in the resolution.

If you are using a non-PostScript printer but will be sending your files for typesetting with a Postscript-driven typesetter, make sure you have installed two printer width tables: the HPLaserJet and PostScript. After selecting the Set Printer Info option under the Options menu heading, choose the Laserjet as your printer. Then, select the PostScript printer width table by entering

C:\VENTURA\POSTSCPT.WID

in the Width Table section of the Set Printer Info. dialog box. Because you chose the HP LaserJet as your printer, you will be able to print in the normal manner. When you choose the PostScript width tables, the space apportioned to each character matches what would be used by a PostScript driven printer.

The resulting output from your laser may not look terrific, but you will be able to see line endings and page breaks. Because character widths vary from printer to printer, even slight width differences can make a large deviation in your output. Remember, if you will be using a typesetter, you are only using the laser printer to create a proof copy of the document, not to create final output. Before sending your chapter to a service bureau, though, remember to change the printer to PostScript.

SELECTING A LASER PRINTER

Keep the following information in mind when choosing a laser printer:

- A PostScript printer offers more definition and variety in output. If your laser printer will be the final output device, consider a PostScript printer if you need many special effects.

- A PostScript printer is driven by the same langauge that drives a Linotronic typesetter. If you plan to use a typesetting service frequently, consider a PostScript printer for easy, accurate proofing.

- For in-house printing and speed, consider an HP PCL printer. The ability to greatly increase RAM (up to 4.5 Megs in HP Laserjet II) offers many possibilities for different typestyles.

- If cost is a factor, the HP price tag is also very attractive.

ADDING FONTS

Ventura also allows you to add a number of fonts. More fonts are rapidly becoming available, and more importantly, the prices for new fonts are falling. Note that adding fonts does take up a significant amount of hard disk space, so be sure you have enough space before you start adding fonts.

For PostScript printers, Adobe Systems offers the best selection of fonts. Adobe fonts are based on commercial typefaces from Allied Corporation. A variety Macintosh-based typefaces is also available. Other companies are planning to introduce non-Macintosh PostScript fonts as well.

For HP LaserJets, Bitstream Inc. Fontware offers the best selection. If you use Fontware with a LaserJet Plus, you can only create up to a 30-point size type, but if you use it with LaserJet Series II, there is no limit to point size. SoftCraft and VS Software also offer typefaces for PCL printers.

Adobe fonts can only be used on PostScript-driven printers. Bitstream's Fontware, however, works with PostScript printers and with HP LaserJets.

SoftCraft and Bitstream also offer programs for creating fonts. Working with Bitstream's installation kit is relatively simple, and the program provides an excellent menu system. Another terrific feature is its ability to estimate the time it will take to create new fonts. The kit also checks for sufficient disk space before it begins generating the new font. The difference between the Bitstream Installation Kit and the Softcraft Fontware Installation Program is that Softcraft provides 19 different character sets. With the Softcraft program, you can even build your own customized symbol sets from Bitstream characters.

Fonts are stored in three different ways. Some fonts are permanently stored in the printer's ROM. When the font has been stored in ROM, it is always available for use. Courier 12-point medium and bold (a 10-pitch type) and 8.5-point Line Printer are stored in the HP LaserJet's ROM. Courier, Helvetica (called Swiss in Ventura), and Times Roman (called Dutch in Ventura) are stored in the Apple LaserWriter's ROM.

Some laser printers offer additional typefaces if you plug in ROM cartridges. So far, this method of storage has only been used on non-PostScript laser printers. In Ventura 1.1, the only font that can be added with a ROM cartridge and used is the F font cartridge from Hewlett-Packard.

The third method of storing fonts is on your floppy or hard disks. Fonts stored on disk are called soft fonts. The amount of space required for these fonts varies, but you will find it nearly impossible to store a library of fonts on your floppy disks. You will need to store them on the hard disk in the Ventura directory for use in Ventura.

When you are adding soft fonts, the first consideration is the typeface itself. Obviously, an Old English style typeface will not be appropriate on a modern, slick design. After you have chosen the typeface, it is then time to decide which character set to use.

The ASCII character set is basic. It offers the standard upper- and lowercase characters but does not include the regular typographic symbols, such as the copyright or registered trademark symbols.

The International character set provided with Ventura is fully depicted in Appendix E of the Ventura reference manual. These special characters are used to create foreign language characters. The Ventura character set also includes typographic symbols.

The PC character set includes all the symbols included on your personal computer keyboard. The Roman-8 set is used by Hewlett-Packard and provides many currency symbols as well as non-English language characters. This character set also lacks typographic symbols. The Symbol set is used for math and scientific expressions and is comprised of the Greek alphabet.

One low-end font generator deserves mention as well. Glyphix from SWFTE International allows you to select a typeface, point size, degree of slanting, fill pattern, weight, and orientation. Glyphix then produces a sample of the font, and if you like it, will store it for use on your hard disk. When used with the HP LaserJet, Glyphix adds much versatility to your printer and to Ventura.

THE VENTURA FONTS

Ventura stores font information in three types of files: printer font files, screen font files, and width tables. In order to make better use of Ventura fonts, first consider the functions of each file type.

Printer Font Files

This file contains the data the printer needs to actually print a soft font. When printing begins, Ventura automatically downloads the printer font files used in your chapter. These files are stored in the Ventura directory on your hard disk. If you are using a non-PostScript printer, a printer font file for each type size used must be downloaded. If you are using a PostScript-driven printer, only the outline information, contained in one file, is downloaded.

Screen Font Files

Your computer screen has a low resolution, particularly when compared to the 300 dpi of a laser printer. Ventura's screen fonts cause the fonts to be displayed on screen similar to the way they will appear when printed. The information Ventura uses to make and display the fonts you see on your screen is stored in the screen font files.

Note: not every soft font you purchase and use with Ventura will have a matching screen font. If you do not have a screen font for a typeface, Ventura automatically substitutes a screen font that is installed and is the closest to the selected font.

Width Table Files

The width table files allow Ventura to provide the WYSIWYG (What-You-See-Is-What-You-Get) feature on screen.

You can set Ventura to automatically adjust and justify your text. In order to do so, Ventura must know the exact width of each character. For example, the uppercase "W" is obviously wider than the lowercase "i." Ventura needs this width information to make the automatic adjustment, and the information about each character's width is stored in the width table files. Both the printer font files and the screen font files refer to the width table files used to adjust the text on the page and on the computer screen. You can set the appropriate width information by selecting the Set Printer Info option under the Options menu heading and selecting or building the appropriate width table.

DOWNLOADING FONTS TO A LASER PRINTER

After you have created your soft fonts, you must send them to the laser printer. Because soft fonts are not stored in the laser printer, they must be **downloaded** to the printer, a function Ventura automatically performs at the beginning of the print process.

You can turn this automatic download process off. If you first download your fonts into the laser printer (assuming you have enough printer RAM to hold your fonts), you will avoid waiting for Ventura to download the fonts each time before you actually begin printing. Using the utilities provided by the manufacturer of your printer, download the fonts into your printer and make them permanent before running Ventura. Then, when you want to print Ventura chapters that use these fonts, select the Add/Remove Fonts menu option under the Options menu heading. In the Add/Remove fonts dialog box, the last options on the Style selection block are Download and Resident. Select Resident for these fonts.

If you are using a PostScript-driven printer, you need not specify point size because the font outlines are downloaded into the PostScript printer, and these outlines are used for any point size used in your Ventura chapter. If you are using a non-PostScript-driven printer, each point size used in your chapter must be downloaded.

SoftCraft, VS Software, and SWFTE all have programs that can download the soft fonts. Adding these programs to a start-up batch file can save time by helping you automate the printing process.

ACCELERATOR BOARDS

If you are using the HP LaserJet II, you can add an accelerator board to your laser printer. The following accelerator boards on the market deserve to be mentioned.

The QMS JetScript, the LaserMaster CAPCard, and Tall Tree Systems JLaser Plus are all recommended. These products speed up the LaserJet and offer a wide variety of fonts. Their extra RAM (more than a megabyte) makes these boards a worthwhile investment. The JetScript also converts your HP LaserJet into a PostScript-driven printer.

The LaserMaster Corporation CAPCard package includes two accelerator boards (one for the computer and one for the printer), a connecting cable, software, and an easy-to-read, easy-to-understand manual. Unless you are the type of computer user who keeps a screwdriver handy in your desk drawer, you may not relish the idea of opening your HP LaserJet and tinkering with it. Fear not. LaserMaster's CAPCard is quite easy to install in both the computer and printer.

The results are worth the effort. Speed is not just improved but is phenomenal. Graphic-intense pages that took minutes to produce without CAPCard can be delivered in seconds.

CAPCard provides many other benefits, as well. For example, you can print up to 256 points with the CAPCard installed. More importantly, it enables you to use fonts from other vendors, such as Bitstream Fontware.

If you decide to install the LaserMaster CAPCard, you will wonder how you ever used Ventura and your LaserJet without it. It is an outstanding product for desktop publishers using an HP LaserJet with Ventura.

All the products mentioned here are relatively easy to install. Check with your dealer to make sure there are no compatibility problems with your computer configuration before you purchase any accelerator. Adding one of these boards is a smart investment. The time you save will save you money.

CHAPTER 7

DESIGN

Just as it takes terrific writing to produce great novels, it takes terrific design to create great desktop publishing. No topic in this book is more important; poor design will ruin everything else you've worked for. Learning to operate a computer will not make you a master of design; becoming design-conscious will. Striving to develop better design should be your constant goal.

EXAMPLE: WHAT NOT TO DO WITH VENTURA

It is not easy to make poorly designed documents using Ventura, but it can be done. Consider the example document in Figure 7.1.

The document's problem areas include the following: uneven columns, an oversized gutter, and overbearing border, multiple typefaces on the same line, too many different typefaces overall, underemphasis of important elements with small type, improper leading, and hyphenation of key words in the heading. Note the lack of emphasis in the words "Advertising Campaign," which are the basis for the entire report. This report appears to be hastily assembled, is difficult to read, and has a poor overall design.

ADVERTISING CAMPAIGN

THE **JOLLIE MOLLIE** PROMOTION

for

THE *TWISTER PRETZELS* SNACK

Prepared for the **PENNSYLVANIA** *FOOD CORPORATION*

AN OVERVIEW:

In April, a new snack food will be introduced and marketed by the Pennsylvania Food Corporation. This new product line, The Twister Pretzels Snack, will be extensively marketed nationwide. In order to kick off the campaign, an advertising and promotional strategy will be instituted. This report submits our conclusion and recommendation to use the Jollie Mollie Promotion.

TEST MARKETING RESULTS:

The Twister Pretzels Snack has been test marketed in Harrisburg, Pennsylvania, Atlanta, Georgia, Weatherford, Texas, and Las Vegas, Nevada. The results from consumer surveys have remained constant: The Twister Pretzel Snack is tasty and delicious. However, consumers stated repeatedly that although they would repurchase the product, the name recognition of the snack is unlikely to be retained. Accordingly, we feel repeat sales would diminish unless some sort of instant name recognition is developed and associated with The Twister Pretzel Snack.

We have considered various possible promotions. By an overall consensus of the evaluation committee in the Marketing Department, we firmly believe the Jollie Mollie Promotion is the strongest concept developed. We strongly recommend and urge the use of the Jollie Mollie Promotion to develop the name recognition we need for our new Twister Pretzel Snack product line.

THE JOLLIE MOLLIE PROMOTION

The Jollie Mollie Promotion consists of using a Boxer dog, named Jollie Mollie, as our advertising mascot. Jollie Mollie, the Boxer Dog, would rather eat a Twister Pretzel Snack, than her dog food. And she would do anything for a Twister Pretzel Snack, including the twister, a special dog dance where she twists and jumps with joy in the anticipation of eating a Twister Pretzel Snack.

We see immense possibilities with an advertising campaign such as this. Cute animals have successively worked in the past in advertising promotions. We see no reason why the Jollie Mollie concept will not enjoy immense, and instant acceptance by the public.

We see the Jollie Mollie advertising attracting public attention quickly. We recommend the use of Twister music, a spin off from the old Twist dance music. When ever the music starts, we will normally see a crowded room, in a party atmosphere. In the center of the happy group will be Jollie Mollie, doing her Twist in anticipation of the Twister Pretzel Snack.

POSSIBLE NEGATIVE CONCEPTS

We did express two concerns over using a dog in our campaign. We wanted to make certain that we received no adverse publicity for feeding a dog pretzels over its regular dog food. For that reason, we will never show Jollie Mollie actually eating a Twister Pretzel Snack. Secondly, we did not want our pretzels associated with dog food products. We believe by having people in our advertising actually eating and enjoying the product, this problem will be overcome. We also feel that by using the voice-over announcement at the end of each commercial saying, "Jollie Mollie will do the Twister for a Twister Pretzel Snack. What would you do for a Twister?" will prevent any misdirected product identification.

We also agreed that other companies, most notably a brewing company selling beer, used a dog successfully in their advertising campaigns. And in our research, we found no indication that anyone complained about a dog drinking alcoholic beverages. We did note, however, that some schools were complaining about the effectiveness of the advertising, and were fearful that the dog was promoting beer drinking among the young. We reiterate our belief that by using a dog as our lead in the promotion of the product, instant name recognition will be built.

THE JOLLIE MOLLIE LOGO

We feel there should be an all-out effort to promote Jollie Mollie. Personal appearances at retail stores, malls, and distributors throughout the nation, Jollie-Mollie T-Shirts and baseball caps (available through mail order and by using an order form on our package), the Jollie Mollie fan club, and even a contest, "What I'd do for a Twister!" should be started.

We think the likeness of Jollie Mollie should be included on our package, on our trucks, and on all ad displays provided to the retailers.

What not to do with Ventura

Figure 7.1

STYLE SHEETS

Because one of the most important aspects of mastering Ventura is good design, one of Ventura's strongest features is **style sheets**. The 25 style sheets included with Ventura are examples of good design. Design problems can develop when Ventura users stray from the provided style sheets.

You can, however, experiment with new designs and use style sheets other than those provided with Ventura. Just as it is possible to create poorly designed documents with Ventura, it is also possible to create new and exciting designs.

Because Ventura can accommodate large fonts and so many different fonts on a single page, some desktop publishers choose to include them all in a single document. What your PC and Ventura can accomplish may be impressive, but using excessive fonts is poor design practice.

Placing design power in the hands of a non-design-oriented person can also create problems. Few people—except graphic designers—have design and graphics experience. With desktop publishing, writers and editors—before concerned only with choosing the right words—must now become desktop publishers, and being a desktop publisher means being a graphic designer.

An obvious solution is to hire a graphic designer. If you choose to hire an expert designer, make sure he or she can use Ventura. Your designer should create your new design *and* a new style sheet.

Another option is to design your own document and style sheet, which is probably what you will be doing. After all, one reason to become a desktop publisher is to have total design control.

Examine other printed pieces—both appreciatively *and* critically. If you admire other work, ask yourself why a particular design appeals to you. Be sure to examine typefaces, use of photos and graphics, the mix of the various page elements, and how much white space (non-printed area) remains on the document. Start a scrapbook or file folder of designs that appeal to you.

Next, build upon other designs. If another design appeals to you, try to duplicate it with Ventura. A good design sense is not something you can install in your computer; it is achieved through experience and experimentation.

BASIC DESIGN PRINCIPLES

Design experimentation should be fun, but you should keep in mind many principles as you begin to create designs. Following is a list of suggestions to help you become a better designer:

1. **Choose type styles carefully**. Typefaces determine the personality and tone of your documents. Consider the audience your document will be reaching when choosing a typeface.

2. **Use serif typefaces for body text**. Typefaces with serifs (such as Times Roman—called Dutch in Ventura) should be used for body text to make it easy to read. Even if you have access to an Old English typeface, avoid the temptation to use it for body text; it is just too hard to read.

3. **Use sans-serif typeface for headlines, charts, and tables**. Sans-serif typefaces are ideal for headlines, charts, tables, and captions. If you must mix typefaces, use sans-serif for headlines and captions and use serif typefaces for major portions of text.

4. **Use typefaces to create a format**. If you are creating a book, use the same typeface and point size for all chapter headings. Use the same typeface for body text throughout the book, and use the same typeface for headlines. By doing so, you create a consistent format.

likely to be retained. Accordingly, we feel repeat sales would diminish unless some sort of instant name recognition is developed and associated with The Twister Pretzel Snack.

We have considered various possible promotions. By an overall consensus of the evaluation committee in the Marketing Department, we firmly believe the Jollie Mollie Promotion is the strongest concept developed. We strongly recommend and urge the use of the Jollie Mollie Promotion to develop the name recognition we need for our new Twister Pretzel Snack product line.

THE JOLLIE MOLLIE PROMOTION

The Jollie Mollie Promotion consists of using a Boxer dog, named Jollie Mollie, as our advertising mascot. Jollie Mollie, the Boxer Dog, would rather eat a Twister Pretzel Snack, than her dog food. And she would do anything for a Twister Pretzel Snack, including the twister, a special dog dance where she twists and jumps with joy in the anticipation of eating a Twister Pretzel Snack.

We see immense possibilities with an advertising campaign such as this. Cute animals have successively worked in the past in advertising promotions. We see no reason why the Jollie Mollie concept will not enjoy immense, and instant acceptance by the public.

We see the Jollie Mollie advertising attracting public attention quickly. We recommend the use of Twister music, a spin off from the old Twist dance music. When ever the music starts, we will normally see a crowded room, in a party atmosphere. In the center of the happy group will be Jollie Mollie, doing her Twist in anticipation of the Twister Pretzel Snack.

POSSIBLE NEGATIVE CONCEPTS

We did express two concerns over using a dog in our campaign. We wanted to make certain that we received no adverse publicity for feeding a dog pretzels over its regular dog food. For that reason, we will never show Jollie Mollie actually eating a Twister Pretzel Snack. Secondly, we did not want our pretzels associated with dog food products. We believe by having people in our advertising actually eating and enjoying the product, this problem will be overcome. We also feel that by using the voice-over announcement at the end of each commercial saying, "Jollie Mollie will do the Twister for a Twister Pretzel Snack. What would you do for a Twister?" will prevent any misdirected product identification.

Use the same type styles for similar elements. The lines "The Jollie Mollie Promotion" and "Possible Negative Concepts" should be in the same type style.

Figure 7.2

5. **Avoid using many typefaces in a single document**. Even if your library includes over 100 different typefaces, avoid the temptation to use them all in a document. No more than two or three different typefaces should be used in any one document.

6. **Use boldface type style for authority**. The very nature of bold type creates an impression of authority.

7. **Use italics to add emphasis**. Words underlined in typewritten text should be italicized when typeset. Italics add emphasis in a subtle, non-obtrusive way.

8. **Use bold-italic to create a feeling of movement**. The combination of bold and italic gives the reader a sense of movement or action. Use this combination to convey a feeling of motion.

9. **Do not mix typefaces**. Use only one typeface per line. Don't mix them, or your finished product will resemble a ransom note.

10. **Vary point sizes for different types of text.** Body text should be set in a smaller typeface than headlines and subheadings. Adjust the size of text to indicate its importance within the document.

(See Figure 7.3 on next page)

ADVERTISING CAMPAIGN

THE JOLLIE MOLLIE PROMOTION

FOR

THE TWISTER PRETZELS SNACK

Prepared for the
PENNSYLVANIA FOOD CORPORATION

AN OVERVIEW:

In April, a new snack food will be introduced and marketed by the Pennsylvania Food Corporation. This new product line, The Twister Pretzels Snack, will be extensively marketed nationwide. In order to kick off the campaign, an advertising and promotional strategy will be instituted. This report submits our conclusion and recommendation to use the Jollie Mollie Promotion.

TEST MARKETING RESULTS:

The Twister Pretzels Snack has been test marketed in Harrisburg, Pennsylvania, Atlanta, Georgia, Weatherford, Texas, and Las Vegas, Nevada. The results from consumer surveys have remained constant: The Twister Pretzel Snack is tasty and delicious. However, consumers stated repeatedly that although they would repurchase the product, the name recognition of the snack is unlikely to be retained. Accordingly, we feel repeat sales would diminish unless some sort of instant name recognition is developed and associated with The Twister Pretzel Snack.

We have considered various possible promotions. By an overall consensus of the evaluation committee in the Marketing Department, we firmly believe the Jollie Mollie Promotion is the strongest concept developed. We strongly recommend and urge the use of the Jollie Mollie Promotion to develop the name recognition we need for our new Twister Pretzel Snack product line.

THE JOLLIE MOLLIE PROMOTION

The Jollie Mollie Promotion consists of using a Boxer dog, named Jollie Mollie, as our advertising mascot. Jollie Mollie, the Boxer Dog, would rather eat a Twister Pretzel Snack, than her dog food. And she would do anything for a Twister Pretzel Snack, including

If the same point size used for body text is used for headlines, the text looks bland, and there is no emphasis associated with the headline text.

Figure 7.3

11. **Be consistent**. Use the same typefaces and point sizes consistently throughout your publication. Don't change typefaces for headlines, subheads, or captions.

12. **Do not use long lines of text in your document**. If a line of type is too long, the reader's eye loses track, jumps from the line, and tries to find the beginning of the next line. A line of text should be no longer than approximately 1.5 times the length of the alphabet—about 40 characters.

13. **Use proper type size for your headlines**. Headlines should stand out and be larger than body text, but the headline should not distract from the masthead (master heading). Headlines should be large enough so that they can be easily read.

NOTICE

The Third Annual
Company Picnic

will be held

Saturday, July 19

Rain or Shine

Proper use of type size arranges the importance of elements for your reader. Improper use of type size confuses them. In this example, the least important line has been overemphasized.

Figure 7.4

NOTICE

The Third Annual Company Picnic

will be held

Saturday, July 19

•

Rain or Shine

Compare this notice with the example in Figure 7.4. Clearly, the proper use of type size catches the reader's attention in this figure.

Figure 7.5

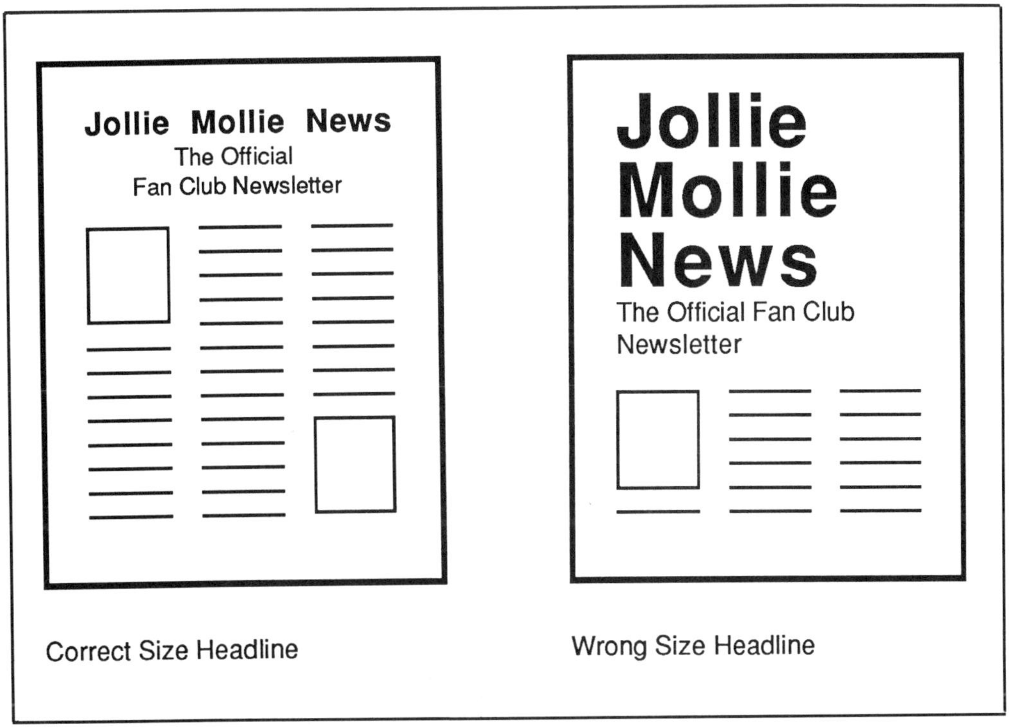

Choosing the correct type size for headlines is important. Notice how the correct headline adds to the page composition, and the oversized headline detracts from the page appearance.

Figure 7.6

ADVERTISING
CAMPAIGN

THE JOLLIE MOLLIE
PROMOTION

FOR

THE TWISTER
PRETZELS SNACK

Prepared for the
PENNSYLVANIA FOOD
CORPORATION

AN OVERVIEW:

In April, a new snack food will be introduced and marketed by the Pennsylvania Food Corporation. This new product line, The

The type sizes used here overpower the page. They are simply too large for the page size.

Figure 7.7

The Jollie Mollie Promotion consists of using a Boxer dog, named Jollie Mollie, as our advertising mascot. Jollie Mollie, the Boxer Dog, would rather eat a Twister Pretzel Snack, than her dog food. And she would do anything for a Twister Pretzel Snack, including the twister, a special dog dance where she twists and jumps with joy in the anticipation of eating a Twister Pretzel Snack.

We see immense possibilities with an advertising campaign such as this. Cute animals have successively worked in the past in advertising promotions. We see no reason why the Jollie Mollie concept will not enjoy immense, and instant acceptance by the public.

We see the Jollie Mollie advertising attracting public attention quickly. We recommend the use of Twister music, a spin off from the old Twist dance music. When ever the music starts, we will normally see a crowded room, in a party atmosphere. In the center of the happy group will be Jollie Mollie, doing her Twist in anticipation of the Twister Pretzel Snack.

POSSIBLE NEGATIVE CONCEPTS

We did express two concerns over using a dog in our campaign. We wanted to make certain that we received no adverse publicity for feeding a dog pretzels over its regular dog food. For that reason, we will never show Jollie Mollie actually eating a Twister Pretzel Snack. Secondly, we did not want our pretzels associated with dog food products. We believe by having people in our advertising actually eating and enjoying the product, this problem will be overcome. We also feel that by using the voice-over announcement at the end of each commercial saying, "Jollie Mollie will do the Twister for a Twister Pretzel Snack. What would you do for a Twister?" will prevent any misdirected product identification.

We also agreed that other companies, most notably a brewing company selling beer, used a dog successfully in their advertising campaigns. And in our research, we found no indication that anyone complained about a dog drinking alcoholic beverages. We

In this example, the headline is too overpowering for the text.

Figure 7.8

The Jollie Mollie Promotion consists of using a Boxer dog, named Jollie Mollie, as our advertising mascot. Jollie Mollie, the Boxer Dog, would rather eat a Twister Pretzel Snack, than her dog food. And she would do anything for a Twister Pretzel Snack, including the twister, a special dog dance where she twists and jumps with joy in the anticipation of eating a Twister Pretzel Snack.

We see immense possibilities with an advertising campaign such as this. Cute animals have successively worked in the past in advertising promotions. We see no reason why the Jollie Mollie concept will not enjoy immense, and instant acceptance by the public.

We see the Jollie Mollie advertising attracting public attention quickly. We recommend the use of Twister music, a spin off from the old Twist dance music. When ever the music starts, we will normally see a crowded room, in a party atmosphere. In the center of the happy group will be Jollie Mollie, doing her Twist in anticipation of the Twister Pretzel Snack.

POSSIBLE NEGATIVE CONCEPTS

We did express two concerns over using a dog in our campaign. We wanted to make certain that we received no adverse publicity for feeding a dog pretzels over its regular dog food. For that reason, we will never show Jollie Mollie actually eating a Twister Pretzel Snack. Secondly, we did not want our pretzels associated with dog food products. We believe by having people in our advertising actually eating and enjoying the product, this problem will be overcome. We also feel that by using the voice-over announcement at the end of each commercial saying, "Jollie Mollie will do the Twister for a Twister Pretzel Snack. What would you do for a Twister?" will prevent any misdirected product identification.

We also agreed that other companies, most notably a brewing company selling beer, used a dog successfully in their advertising campaigns. And in our research, we found no indication that anyone complained about a dog drinking alcoholic beverages. We did note, however, that some schools were complaining about the effectiveness of the advertising, and were fearful that the dog was promoting beer drinking among the young. We reiterate our belief that by using a dog as our lead in the promotion of the product, instant name recognition will be built.

THE JOLLIE MOLLIE LOGO

We feel there should be an all-out effort to promote Jollie Mollie. Personal appearances at retail stores, malls, and distributors

The headlines here are the same size as the body text. Using uppercase makes them look bigger, but they still do not stand out as well as they could if a larger type size was used.

Figure 7.9

14. **Use both upper- and lowercase in your headlines.** Unless your headlines are very short (such as WE DID IT!), use both upper- and lowercase text in your headlines. Uppercase letters in longer headlines become hard to read.

USING ONLY UPPER CASE TYPE CAN MAKE YOUR TEXT HARDER TO READ. **Use both upper and lower case type. Experts agree that upper and lower case type creates word pictures, and are easier to read. This is especially true for your body text.**

Note the difference between these two brief examples. Your eyes will naturally slow down when reading all uppercase text. It is easier to read the upper-and-lowercase text.

Figure 7.10

15. **Use strong, descriptive, tightly packed words in headlines.** Spend time working on your headlines. As already described, your headlines are an extremely important element of the overall design of your document. Consider the impact of the following two headlines:

Police Kill House Burglar

Local Police Officers Shoot Suspect Breaking and Entering A Home

Although the second headline provides more detail, the first headline has more impact. This concept may seem to have more to do with writing than design, but the overall design of a document will be adversely affected by poorly written, poorly composed headlines.

16. **Use logical breaks in headlines.** A long line of text in a headline that has been broken into two lines must make sense and be easy to read. Consider the following headline:

Police Arrest Drunk
Driver In Jail

What really happened? Were the police drunk when they arrested a driver in jail, or did the police arrest a drunk driver who happened to be in jail? Always consider what your headline might be saying when you break a headline into more than one line.

17. **Use subheads effectively**. Headlines grabs a reader's attention. Subheads should visually take readers from the headline into the body text and introduce a more specific topic. The headline should be large; the subhead should be smaller than the headline; and the body text should be smaller than the subhead.

18. **Use proper leading**. With too much or too little space between lines, text can be hard to read. Choose the right amount of **leading** for your text lines.

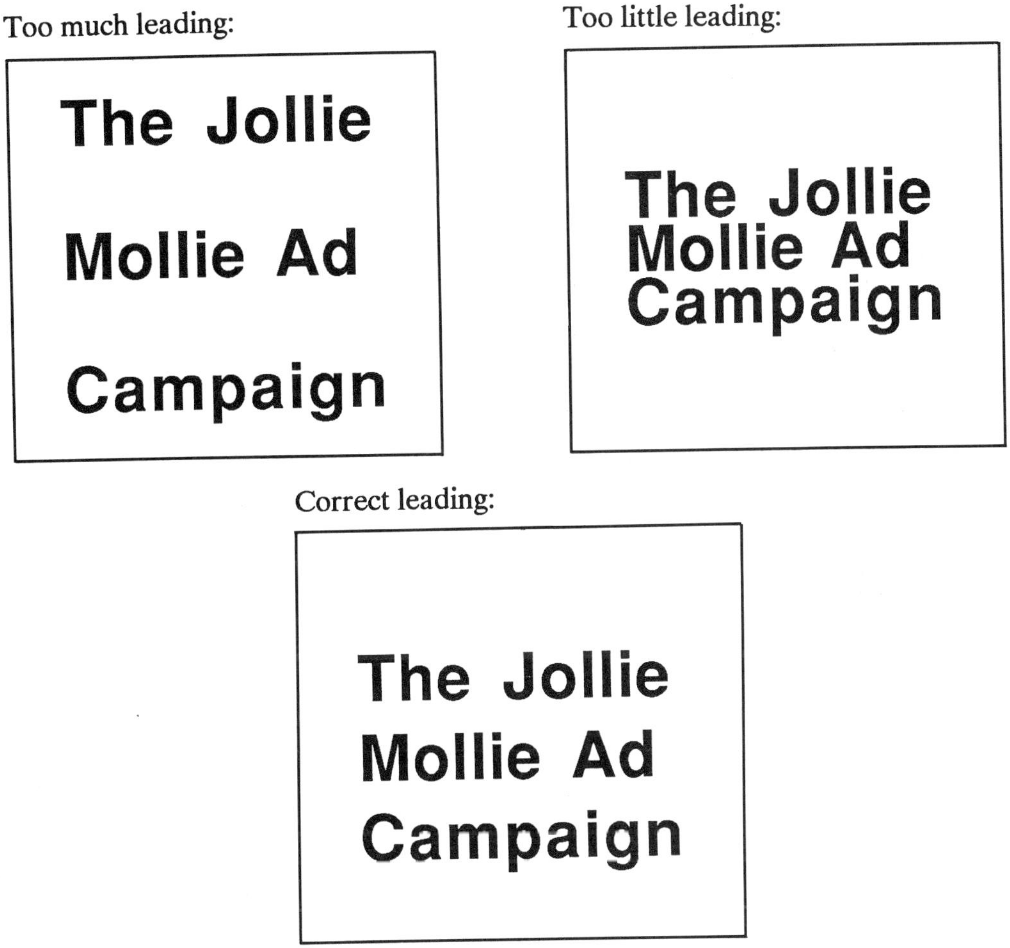

Proper leading is important. Notice how the correct leading ties the elements of each line together while either too much or too little leading makes text difficult to read.

Figure 7.11

We have considered various possible promotions. By an overall consensus of the evaluation committee in the Marketing Department, we firmly believe the Jollie Mollie Promotion is the strongest concept developed. We strongly recommend and urge the use of the Jollie Mollie Promotion to develop the name recognition we need for our Twister Pretzel Snack product line.

The Jollie Mollie Promotion consists of using a Boxer dog, named Jollie Mollie, as our advertising mascot. Jollie Mollie, the Boxer Dog, would rather eat a Twister Pretzel Snack, than her dog food. And she would do anything for a Twister Pretzel Snack, including the twister, a special dog dance where she twists and jumps with joy in the anticipation of eating a Twister Pretzel Snack.

We see immense possibilities with an advertising campaign such as this. Cute animals have successively worked in the past in advertising promotions. We see no reason why the Jollie Mollie concept will not enjoy immense, and instant acceptance by the public. We see the Jollie Mollie advertising attracting public attention quickly.

We recommend the use of Twister music, a spin off from the old Twist dance music. When ever the music starts, we will normally see a crowded room, in a party atmosphere. In the center of the happy group will be Jollie Mollie, doing her Twist in anticipation of the Twister Pretzel Snack.

Figure 7.12 is an example of 12-point type used with 9-point leading. Too little space makes this text difficult to read. It makes type look packed, cramped.

Figure 7.12

We have considered various possible promotions. By an overall consensus of the evaluation committee in the Marketing Department, we firmly believe the Jollie Mollie Promotion is the strongest concept developed. We strongly recommend and urge the use of the Jollie Mollie Promotion to develop the name recognition we need for our Twister Pretzel Snack product line.

The Jollie Mollie Promotion consists of using a Boxer dog, named Jollie Mollie, as our advertising mascot. Jollie Mollie, the Boxer Dog, would rather eat a Twister Pretzel Snack, than her dog food. And she would do anything for a Twister Pretzel Snack, including the twister, a special dog dance where she twists and jumps with joy in the anticipation of eating a Twister Pretzel Snack.

Figure 7.13 is an example of 12-point type used with 24-point leading. Excessive leading separates the lines with too much white space, making text difficult to read.

Figure 7.13

We have considered various possible promotions. By an overall consensus of the evaluation committee in the Marketing Department, we firmly believe the Jollie Mollie Promotion is the strongest concept developed. We strongly recommend and urge the use of the Jollie Mollie Promotion to develop the name recognition we need for our Twister Pretzel Snack product line.

The Jollie Mollie Promotion consists of using a Boxer dog, named Jollie Mollie, as our advertising mascot. Jollie Mollie, the Boxer Dog, would rather eat a Twister Pretzel Snack, than her dog food. And she would do anything for a Twister Pretzel Snack, including the twister, a special dog dance where she twists and jumps with joy in the anticipation of eating a Twister Pretzel Snack.

We see immense possibilities with an advertising campaign such as this. Cute animals have successively worked in the past in advertising promotions. We see no reason why the Jollie Mollie concept will not enjoy immense, and instant acceptance by the public. We see the Jollie Mollie advertising attracting public attention quickly.

Figure 7.14 is an example of correct leading. The text was set in 12-point type with 14-point leading. Notice how easy the text is to read.

Figure 7.14

19. **Use white space effectively**. Desktop publishers often try to fill a page with type, text, line art, and graphics. Do not fall into that trap: use white space to make your designs better, cleaner, and more effective. White space adds a natural border to a page and helps whatever it surrounds stand out.

20. **Do not use white space in the middle of a page**. Although white space is an effective design aid, it should not be used in the center of a page because it creates an unnatural hole.

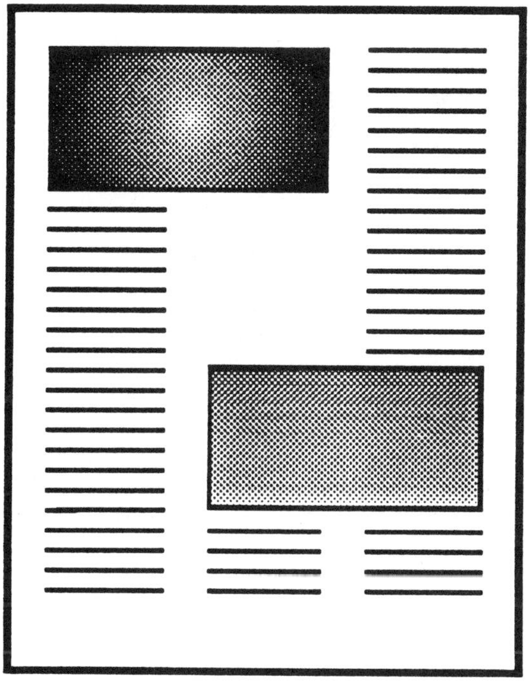

White space trapped in the middle of the page. This problem most often occurs in layouts containing graphics.

Figure 7.15

21. **Use white space to make headlines stand out**. Effectively surrounding headlines with white space can give them added impact.

ment, we firmly believe the Jollie Mollie Promotion is the strongest concept developed. We strongly recommend and urge the use of the Jollie Mollie Promotion to develop the name recognition we need for our new Twister Pretzel Snack product line.

THE JOLLIE MOLLIE PROMOTION

The Jollie Mollie Promotion consists of using a Boxer dog, named Jollie Mollie, as our advertising mascot. Jollie Mollie, the Boxer Dog, would rather eat a Twister Pretzel Snack, than her dog food. And she would do anything for a Twister Pretzel Snack, including the twister, a special dog dance where she twists and jumps with joy in the anticipation of eating a Twister Pretzel Snack.

We see immense possibilities with an advertising campaign such as this. Cute animals have successively worked in the past in advertising promotions. We see no reason why the Jollie Mollie concept will not enjoy immense, and instant acceptance by the public.

We see the Jollie Mollie advertising attracting public attention quickly. We recommend the use of Twister music, a spin off from the old Twist dance music. When ever the music starts, we will normally see a crowded room, in a party atmosphere. In the center of the happy group will be Jollie Mollie, doing her Twist in anticipation of the Twister Pretzel Snack.

POSSIBLE NEGATIVE CONCEPTS

We did express two concerns over using a dog in our campaign. We wanted to make certain that we received no adverse publicity for feeding a dog pretzels over its regular dog food. For that reason, we will never show Jollie Mollie actually eating a Twister Pretzel Snack. Secondly, we did not want our pretzels associated with dog food products. We believe by having people in our advertising actually eating and enjoying the product, this problem will be overcome. We also feel that by using the voice-over announcement at the end of each commercial saying, "Jollie Mollie will do the Twister for a Twister Pretzel Snack. What would you do for a Twister?" will prevent any misdirected product identification.

We also agreed that other companies, most notably a brewing company selling beer, used a dog successfully in their advertising campaigns. And in our research, we found no indication that anyone complained about a dog drinking alcoholic beverages. We did note, however, that some schools were complaining about the effectiveness of the advertising, and were fearful that the dog was promoting beer drinking among the young. We reiterate our belief that by using a dog as our lead in the promotion of the product, instant name recognition will be built.

The lack of white space between the body text and the headlines makes this page look too packed and unappealing.

Figure 7.16

We have considered various possible promotions. By an overall consensus of the evaluation committee in the Marketing Department, we firmly believe the Jollie Mollie Promotion is the strongest concept developed. We strongly recommend and urge the use of the Jollie Mollie Promotion to develop the name recognition we need for our new Twister Pretzel Snack product line.

THE JOLLIE MOLLIE PROMOTION

The Jollie Mollie Promotion consists of using a Boxer dog, named Jollie Mollie, as our advertising mascot. Jollie Mollie, the Boxer Dog, would rather eat a Twister Pretzel Snack, than her dog food. And she would do anything for a Twister Pretzel Snack, including the twister, a special dog dance where she twists and jumps with joy in the anticipation of eating a Twister Pretzel Snack.

We see immense possibilities with an advertising campaign such as this. Cute animals have successively worked in the past in advertising promotions. We see no reason why the Jollie Mollie concept will not enjoy immense, and instant acceptance by the public.

We see the Jollie Mollie advertising attracting public attention quickly. We recommend the use of Twister music, a spin off from the old Twist dance music. When ever the music starts, we will normally see a crowded room, in a party atmosphere. In the center of the happy group will be Jollie Mollie, doing her Twist in anticipation of the Twister Pretzel Snack.

POSSIBLE NEGATIVE CONCEPTS

We did express two concerns over using a dog in our campaign. We wanted to make certain that we received no adverse publicity for feeding a dog pretzels over its regular dog food. For that reason, we will never show Jollie Mollie actually eating a Twister Pretzel Snack. Secondly, we did not want our pretzels associated with dog food products. We believe by having people in our advertising actually eating and enjoying the product, this problem will be overcome. We also feel that by using the voice-over announcement at the end of each commercial saying, "Jollie Mollie will do the Twister for a Twister Pretzel Snack. What would you do for a Twister?" will prevent any misdirected product identification.

We also agreed that other companies, most notably a brewing company selling beer, used a dog successfully in their advertising campaigns. And in our research, we found no indication that anyone complained about a dog drinking alcoholic beverages. We did note, however, that some schools were complaining about the effectiveness of the advertising, and were fearful that the dog was promoting beer drinking among the young. We reiterate our belief that by using

Notice how proper white space sets off the page elements.

Figure 7.17

22. **Use sufficient white space as a natural margin.** By using white space as a natural margin, you frame your document's design. White space forces the reader's eyes to the center of the page.

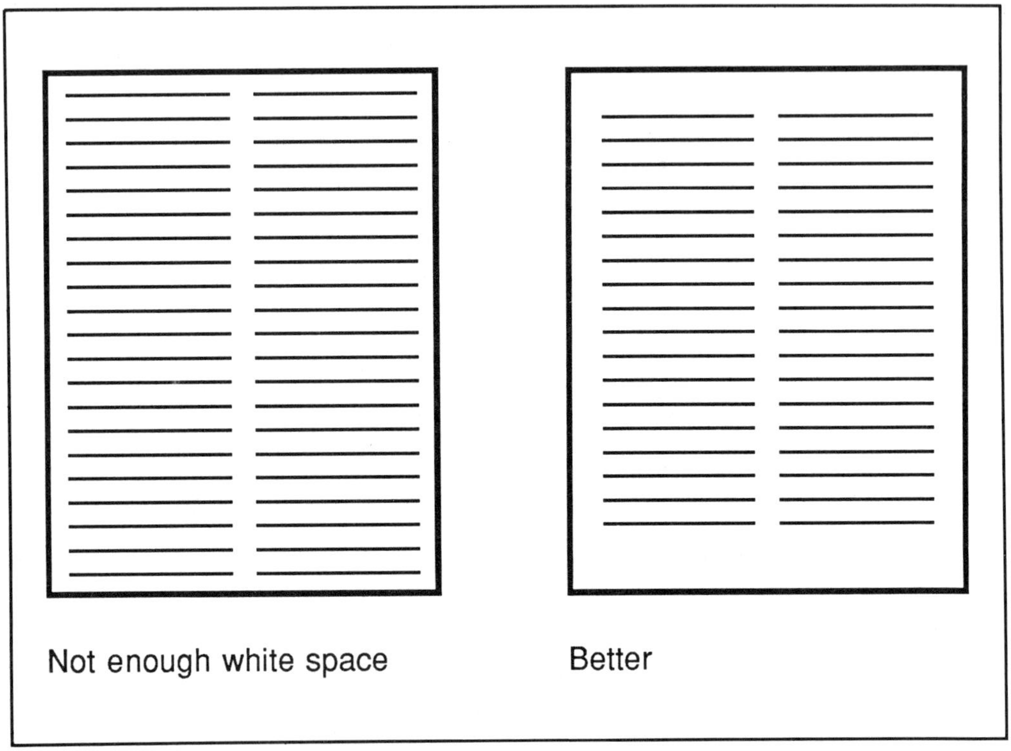

Proper margins are important for good design. Use plenty of white space for margins.

Figure 7.18

23. **Use white space to add balance.** Sometimes a large headline, oversized photo, or special graphic is needed. White space helps achieve the necessary balance.

24. **Overuse of white space.** If one design element cannot be overused in your designs, it is natural white space. The more white space, in most cases, the better your design will be.

likely to be retained. Accordingly, we feel repeat sales would diminish unless some sort of instant name recognition is developed and associated with The Twister Pretzel Snack.

We have considered various possible promotions. By an overall consensus of the evaluation committee in the Marketing Department, we firmly believe the Jollie Mollie Promotion is the strongest concept developed. We strongly recommend and urge the use of the Jollie Mollie Promotion to develop the name recognition we need for our new Twister Pretzel Snack product line.

THE JOLLIE MOLLIE PROMOTION

The Jollie Mollie Promotion consists of using a Boxer dog, named Jollie Mollie, as our advertising mascot. Jollie Mollie, the Boxer Dog, would rather eat a Twister Pretzel Snack, than her dog food. And she would do anything for a Twister Pretzel Snack, including the twister, a special dog dance where she twists and jumps with joy in the anticipation of eating a Twister Pretzel Snack.

We see immense possibilities with an advertising campaign such as this. Cute animals have successively worked in the past in advertising promotions. We see no reason why the Jollie Mollie concept will not enjoy immense, and instant acceptance by the public.

We see the Jollie Mollie advertising attracting public attention quickly. We recommend the use of Twister music, a spin off from the old Twist dance music. When ever the music starts, we will normally see a crowded room, in a party atmosphere. In the center of the happy group will be Jollie Mollie, doing her Twist in anticipation of the Twister Pretzel Snack.

POSSIBLE NEGATIVE CONCEPTS

We did express two concerns over using a dog in our campaign. We wanted to make certain that we received no adverse publicity for feeding a dog pretzels over its regular dog food. For that reason, we will never show Jollie Mollie actually eating a Twister Pretzel Snack. Secondly, we did not want our pretzels associated with dog food products. We believe by having people in our advertising actually eating and enjoying the product, this problem will be overcome. We also feel that by using the voice-over announcement at the end of each commercial saying, "Jollie Mollie will do the Twister

Compare this example with previous examples displaying this page. Note how each problem has been eliminated, even with this simple design.

Figure 7.19

25. **Use bullets to indicate separate points**. Bullets add emphasis and indicate that each text entry represents a separate, distinct point.

26. **Add boxes to an all-text page**. When preparing an all-text page, place a box in it to break the page's monotony. The box can contain a **lift** (a sentence or two of significant body text). Boxes can also contain a chart or other related text.

27. **Position a box slightly above center**. A box, no matter what it contains, will usually look best if positioned slightly above center on an otherwise all-text page.

28. **Make the box appealing**. There are several techniques—such as screening, reversing, or shadowing—to make a box more appealing.

29. **Frame boxes with thin ruled lines**. Thick ruled lines detract from a box's contents. Use thin rule lines to make a more attractive box.

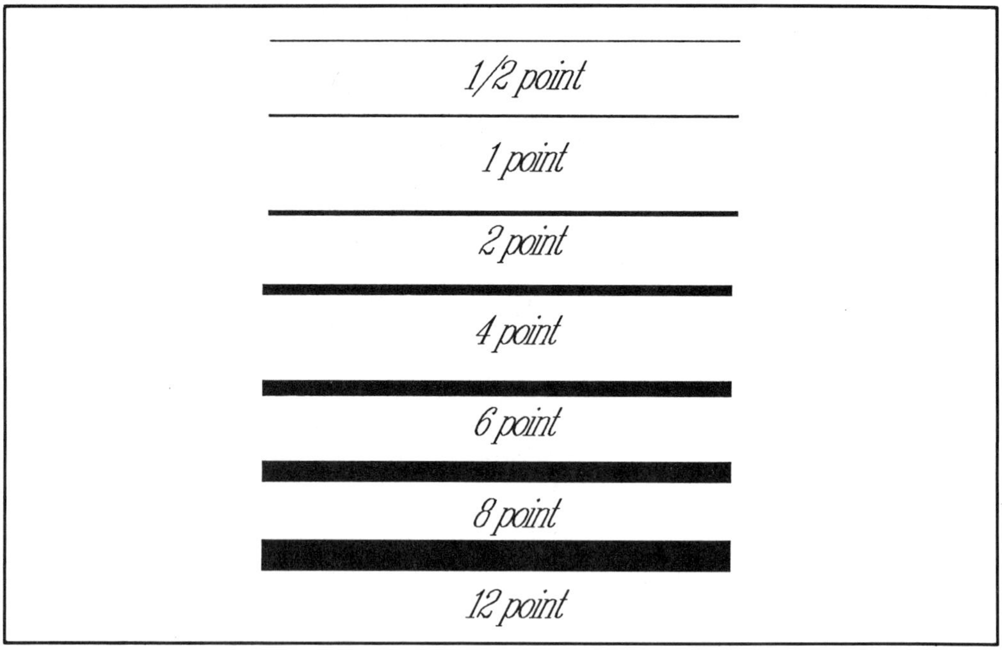

Avoid thick rules. Often, thinner rules add and enhance the design. Thick rules overpower and detract from the design. This chart compares the various thicknesses of ruling lines.

Figure 7.20

30. **Use standard margins**. Set margins at the beginning of your document, and maintain standard margins throughout the document. Do not change margins from one page to another.

31. **Make inside margins larger if your document will be bound**. If your document is to be stapled or bound, add additional inside margin space so the text is not affected. This technique requires a larger left margin on the right-side pages and a larger right margin on left-side pages.

32. **Use headers and footers**. Just as you can now tell what chapter and page you are reading in this book, you should keep the reader informed of where he or she is in your document. Use headers and footers to provide that information.

33. **Consider headers and footers when determining margin settings**. If your document contains multiple pages, headers and footers will be needed. Consider their position when developing your document's design.

34. **Make your headers and footers part of the design**. Do not overemphasize headers and footers; they should be part of the document's design. Do not allow a header or footer to intrude on the rest of the text.

35. **Use quote pulls to break up text**. Add quote pulls (quotes pulled from text) to break up all-text pages.

36. **Use quote pulls to emphasize key points**. If you are using a quote pull, make sure it emphasizes an important part of your text.

37. **Use quote pulls to fill columns**. Sometimes, a few inches of unused space will remain in a column, and nothing else will quite fit into that space. Use a quote pull (higher in the text) to help fill the column.

38. **Use side bars**. A **side bar** is a item related to the main subject. It is a mini-article often used to provide different or additional information. For example, if you were publishing an article about desktop publishing, a typical side bar might discuss how to create better desktop publishing documents. Sidebars keep text from becoming long and boring. Also, use a sidebar to help balance your design. The sidebar can be shaded, screened, or framed.

39. **Eliminate widows and orphans**. The best way to eliminate widows and orphans (incomplete lines at the top or bottom of pages, respectively) is to edit the copy or use Ventura's Widows and Orphans feature under the Page menu heading.

40. **Use kerning effectively**. Particularly important in headlines, **kerning** removes unnatural space that sometimes occurs between characters. Kerning brings letters closer together, makes the words easier to read, and improves the document's appearance.

Excessive use of
letterspacing
looks bad. And
it is hard to read
and to com-
prehend. Be
cautious when-
ever you decide
to change the set-
tings of let-
terspacing. If
you are not, you
could create text
that is difficult
to read, and ex-
tremely hard to
understand.

This text is nearly impossible to read because of overspacing between letters.

Figure 7.21

Manual kerning is easy in Ventura. Note the difference between the two words in Figure 7.22. To kern manually in Ventura, enter Text mode (Ctrl/O), and select the letter to be moved to the left. Then select the Set Font option above the side bar under the Paragraph menu heading, and in the Shift section of the Set Font dialog box, enter the amount of space you want to shift. Kerning is needed primarily in large font sizes, particularly in headlines.

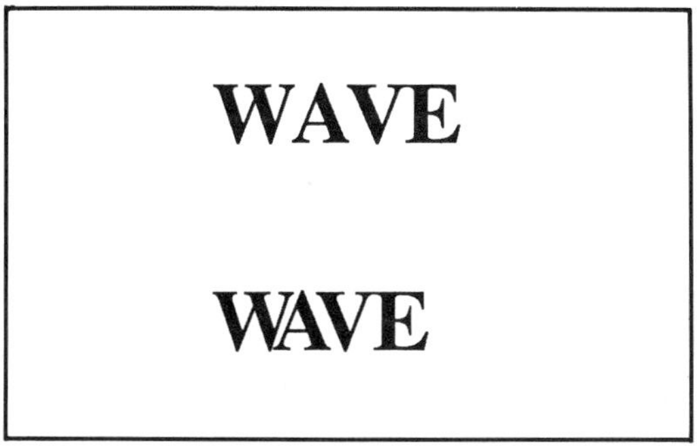

Figure 7.22

41. **Crop photos and art for impact**. Many photos and art items can be more effective and appealing if cropped.

42. **Use columns effectively**. The number of columns in a document is your choice; however, if you are using many columns (three, four, five, or more) use a smaller typeface. You can use a large typeface for fewer columns (one or two). Remember the guideline discussed earlier: approximately 40 characters per line.

In April, a new snack food will be introduced and marketed by the Pennsylvania Food Corporation. This new product line, The Twister Pretzels Snack, will be extensively marketed nationwide. In order to kick off the campaign, an advertising and promotional strategy will be instituted. This report submits our conclusions and recommendation to use the Jollie Mollie Promotion.

TEST MARKETING RESULTS:

The Twister Pretzels Snack has been test marketed in Harrisburg, Pennsylvania, Atlanta, Georgia, Weatherford, Texas, and Las Vegas, Nevada. The results from consumer surveys have remained constant: The Twister Pretzel Snack is tasty and delicious. However, consumers stated repeatedly that although they would repurchase the product, the name recognition of the snack is unlikely to be retained. Accordingly, we feel repeat sales would diminish unless some sort of instant name recognition is developed

Overly large type size in columns creates a confusing design. Follow the rule of approximately 35 to 40 characters per line for well-balanced columns.

Figure 7.23

anticipation of eating a Twister Pretzel Snack.

We see immense possibilities with an advertising campaign such as this. Cute animals have successively worked in the past in advertising promotions. We see no reason why the Jollie Mollie concept will not enjoy immense, and instant acceptance by the public.

We see the Jollie Mollie advertising attracting public attention quickly. We recommend the use of Twister music, a spin off from the old Twist dance music. When ever the music starts, we will normally see a crowded room, in a party atmosphere. In the center of the happy group will be Jollie Mollie, doing her Twist in anticipation of the Twister Pretzel Snack.

POSSIBLE NEGATIVE CONCEPTS

We did express two concerns over using a dog in our campaign. We wanted to make certain that we received no adverse publicity for feeding a dog pretzels over its regular dog food. For that reason, we will never show Jollie Mollie actually eating a Twister Pretzel Snack. Secondly, we did not want our pretzels associated with dog food products. We believe by having people in our advertising actually eating and enjoying the product, this problem will be overcome. We also feel that by using the voice-over announceme nt at the end of each commercial saying, "Jollie Mollie will do the Twister for a Twister Pretzel Snack. What would you do for a Twister?" will prevent any misdirected product identification

We also agreed that other companies, most notably a brewing company selling beer, used a dog successfully in their advertising campaigns. And in our research, we found no indication that anyone complained about a dog drinking alcoholic beverages. We did note, however, that some schools were complaining about the effectiveness of the advertising, and were fearful that the dog was promoting beer drinking among the young. We reiterate our belief that by using a dog as our lead in the promotion of the product, instant name recognition will be built.

THE JOLLIE MOLLIE LOGO

We feel there should be an all-out effort to promote Jollie Mollie. Personal appearances at retail stores, malls, and distributors throughout the nation, Jollie-Mollie T-Shirts and baseball caps (available through mail order and by using an order form on our package), the Jollie Mollie fan club, and even a contest, "What I'd do for a Twister!" should be started.

We think the likeness of Jollie Mollie should be included on our package, on our trucks, and on all ad displays provided to the retailers.

We firmly believe that we can create a new national symbol, a new national image, and instant name recognition of the Twister Pretzel Snack.

ADDITIONAL INFORMATIO N:

Included with this report are sample scripts, for

Having too many columns on one page simply doesn't look right. It also creates overly narrow columns, making text extremely difficult to read.

Figure 7.24

worked in the past in advertising promotions. We see no reason why the Jollie Mollie concept will not enjoy immense, and instant acceptance by the public.

We see the Jollie Mollie advertising attracting public attention quickly. We recommend the use of Twister music, a spin off from the old Twist dance music. When ever the music starts, we will normally see a crowded room, in a party atmosphere. In the center of the happy group will be Jollie Mollie, doing her Twist in anticipation of the Twister Pretzel Snack.

POSSIBLE NEGATIVE CONCEPTS

We did express two concerns over using a dog in our campaign. We wanted to make certain that we received no adverse publicity for feeding a dog pretzels over its regular dog food. For that reason, we will never show Jollie Mollie actually eating a Twister Pretzel Snack. Secondly, we did not want our pretzels associated with dog food products. We believe by having people in our advertising actually eating and enjoying the product, this problem will be overcome. We also feel that by using the voice-over announcement at the end of each commercial saying, "Jollie Mollie will do the Twister for a Twister Pretzel Snack. What would you do for a Twister?" will prevent any misdirected product identification.

We also agreed that other companies, most notably a brewing company selling beer, used a dog successfully in their advertising campaigns. And in our research, we found no indication that anyone complained about a dog drinking alcoholic beverages. We did note, however, that some schools were complaining about the effectiveness of the advertising, and were fearful that the dog was promoting beer drinking among the young. We reiterate our belief that by using a dog as our lead in the promotion of the product, instant name recognition will be built.

THE JOLLIE MOLLIE LOGO

We feel there should be an all-out effort to promote Jollie Mollie. Personal appearances at retail stores, malls, and distributors throughout the nation, Jollie-Mollie T-Shirts and baseball caps (available through mail order and by using an order form on our package), the Jollie Mollie fan club, and even a contest, "What I'd do for a Twister!" should be started.

We think the likeness of Jollie Mollie should be included on our package, on our trucks, and on all ad displays provided to the retailers.

We firmly believe that we can create a new national symbol, a new national image, and instant name recognition of the Twister Pretzel Snack.

ADDITIONAL INFORMATION:

Included with this report are sample scripts, for both TV advertising and radio spots, estimated costs for production, promotional plans for the personal appearances of Jollie Mollie, the establishment of the Jollie Mollie fan club, the results of the consumer studies and surveys, the report on other advertising campaigns considered, and why they were rejected. We have also attached other information, such as distribution costs, anticipated profits, costs of advertising, break even and profit

Compare this page with Figures 7.22 and 7.23. The columns are much easier to read, only because a proper type size was chosen for the width of the columns.

Figure 7.25

43. **Use justified text in narrow columns**. Justified text columns look more formal and authoritative. They also save space.

44. **Use uneven column widths for variety**. Mix column widths to provide a different, unique look.

45. **Use hyphenation**. Ventura's hyphenation feature adjusts word spacing by automatically hyphenating words at the end of a line when necessary to avoid awkward spacing. By using hyphenation, less white space will be inserted in justified text, making it easier to read. Hyphenation also saves space and also improves the general appearance of the text.

46. **Achieve effective balance**. Sometimes, perfect balance produces bland results. Although balance is important, sometimes a more effectively designed page is not perfectly balanced.

47. **Consider the effect of design on facing pages**. Although two perfectly designed pages may look quite good on their own, they may not work well together when positioned side by side. Sometimes, it helps to create a single design that incorporates two facing pages.

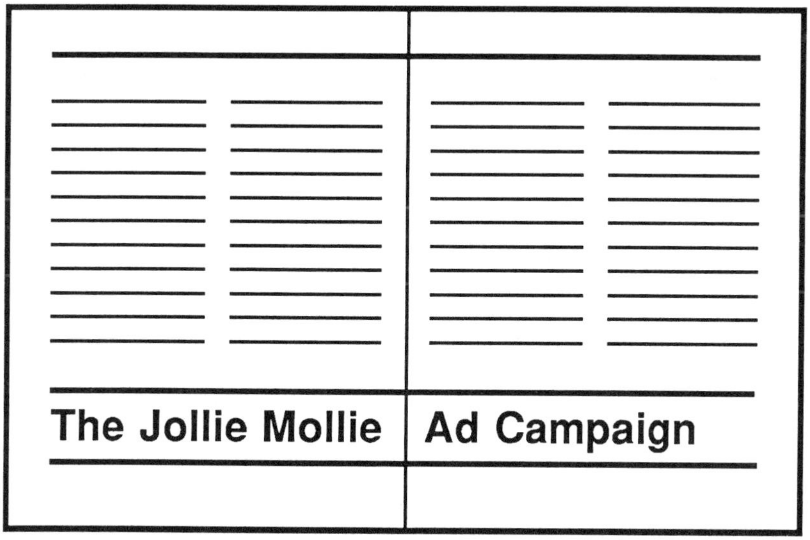

This shows an example of how facing pages can be pulled together with key elements.

Figure 7.26

48. **Use ruled lines**. Lines—vertical and horizontal—help organize and establish a page. Use lines to separate columns, topics, and design elements.

49. **Use different-sized ruled lines**. For balance, thicker ruled lines can be used when more white space is available. Use thinner rules when less white space is available. Double lines can also be used for design variety.

50. **Use art**. Graphs, charts, designs, and illustrations bring life to your words. Use art to make your documents more appealing and to add emphasis.

51. **Use screens**. Screens (blocks of shading) add impact and attract attention.

52. **Add color to your documents**. Adding a touch of color to a document adds impact and authority and provides a fresh look. Use Ventura's color feature to add color to your documents.

53. **When using color, do not use too much.** Too much color detracts from a document. A touch or dash of color—rather than a large amount—will help your document's overall appearance.

54. **Use reverse text**. Reverse text attracts readers' eyes. Use reverse text (white text on a black background) to emphasize a headline or short block of text. When using reverses, use sans-serif typefaces. Do not use serif styles, and do not use small point sizes; they are too hard to read.

55. **Use captions to identify your art and photos.** Captions relate art to body text. Captions must be short and explicit. They should be set in small type and should not interfere with the body text.

56. **Add captions as part of the design**. Captions can be attached to the top, bottom, or sides of the art and can help add balance to a page.

57. **Avoid excesses**. Too much of anything—color, art, rules, special effects—can ruin a document. Following are specific examples:

ADVERTISING CAMPAIGN

THE JOLLIE MOLLIE PROMOTION

for

THE TWISTER PRETZELS SNACK

Prepared for the

PENNSYLVANIA FOOD CORPORATION

AN OVERVIEW:

In April, a new snack food will be introduced and marketed by the Pennsylvania Food Corporation. This new product line, The Twister Pretzels Snack, will be extensively marketed nationwide. In order to kick off the campaign, an advertising and promotional strategy will be instituted. This report submits our conclusion and recommendation to use the Jollie Mollie Promotion.

TEST MARKETING RESULTS:

The Twister Pretzels Snack has been test marketed in Harrisburg, Pennsylvania, Atlanta, Georgia, Weatherford, Texas, and Las Vegas, Nevada. The results from consumer surveys have remained constant: The Twister Pretzel Snack is tasty and delicious. However, consumers stated repeatedly that although they would repurchase the product, the name recognition of the snack is unlikely to be retained. Accordingly, we feel repeat sales would diminish unless some sort of instant name recognition is developed and associated with The Twister Pretzel Snack.

We have considered various possible promotions. By an overall consensus of the evaluation committee in the Marketing Department, we firmly believe the Jollie Mollie Promotion is the strongest concept developed. We strongly recommend and urge the use of the Jollie Mollie Promotion to develop the name recognition we need for our new Twister Pretzel Snack product line.

Adding ruling lines to too many of your paragraph tags can make a page look bad. Do not overuse line elements.

Figure 7.27

ADVERTISING CAMPAIGN

THE JOLLIE MOLLIE PROMOTION

FOR

THE TWISTER PRETZELS SNACK

Prepared for the
PENNSYLVANIA FOOD CORPORATION

AN OVERVIEW:

In April, a new snack food will be introduced and marketed by the Pennsylvania Food Corporation. This new product line, The Twister Pretzels Snack, will be extensively marketed nationwide. In order to kick off the campaign, an advertising and promotional strategy will be instituted. This report submits our conclusion and recommendation to use the Jollie Mollie Promotion.

Removing the ruling lines and adding larger-sized type makes this report look better. Still, the page looks full.

Figure 7.28

ADVERTISING CAMPAIGN

THE JOLLIE MOLLIE PROMOTION

for

THE TWISTER PRETZELS SNACK

Prepared for the PENNSYLVANIA FOOD CORPORATION

AN OVERVIEW:

In April, a new snack food will be introduced and marketed by the Pennsylvania Food Corporation. This new product line, The Twister Pretzels Snack, will be extensively marketed nationwide. In order to kick off the campaign, an advertising and promotional strategy will be instituted. This report submits our conclusion and recommendation to use the Jollie Mollie Promotion.

TEST MARKETING RESULTS:

The Twister Pretzels Snack has been test marketed in Harrisburg, Pennsylvania, Atlanta, Georgia, Weatherford, Texas, and Las Vegas, Nevada. The results from consumer surveys have remained constant: The Twister Pretzel Snack is tasty and delicious. However, consumers stated repeatedly that although they would repurchase the product, the name recognition of the snack is unlikely to be retained. Accordingly, we feel repeat sales would diminish unless some sort of instant name recognition is developed and associated with The Twister Pretzel Snack.

We have considered various possible promotions. By an overall consensus of the evaluation committee in the Marketing Department, we firmly believe the Jollie Mollie Promotion is the strongest concept developed. We strongly recommend and urge the use of the Jollie Mollie Promotion to develop the name recognition we need for our new Twister Pretzel Snack product line.

Compare this example to the previous examples showing this page from the report. By adding white space and down-sizing some of the line elements, the page looks cleaner and is easier to read.

Figure 7.29

58. **Experiment with title or text positions.** Often, the title will be positioned (and centered) on the top of the page. Titles can be positioned on the side, the bottom, or even the middle of a page. On facing pages, titles can cross the span of both pages. Body text can also be centered, right- or left-aligned, or justified.

We have considered various possible promotions. By an overall consensus of the evaluation committee in the Marketing Department, we firmly believe the Jollie Mollie Promotion is the strongest concept developed. We strongly recommend and urge the use of the Jollie Mollie Promotion to develop the name recognition we need for our Twister Pretzel Snack product line.

The Jollie Mollie Promotion consists of using a Boxer dog, named Jollie Mollie, as our advertising mascot. Jollie Mollie, the Boxer Dog, would rather eat a Twister Pretzel Snack, than her dog food. And she would do anything for a Twister Pretzel Snack, including the twister, a special dog dance where she twists and jumps with joy in the anticipation of eating a Twister Pretzel Snack.

We see immense possibilities with an advertising campaign such as this. Cute animals have successively worked in the past in advertising promotions. We see no reason why the Jollie Mollie concept will not enjoy immense, and instant acceptance by the public. We see the Jollie Mollie advertising attracting public attention quickly.

We recommend the use of Twister music, a spin off from the old Twist dance music. When ever the music starts, we will normally see a crowded room, in a party atmosphere. In the center of the happy group will be Jollie Mollie, doing her Twist in anticipation of the Twister Pretzel Snack.

Ventura offers four alignment styles: left, center, right, and justified. Each creates a different visual image.

Figure 7.30

These 58 points are only suggestions. There are no set rules in document design. Be willing to experiment, and be willing to admit when something looks bad. Proofread everything. Check your document, and recheck it before it is sent to the printer for mass production.

CHAPTER 8

THE VENTURA PUBLISHER STYLE SHEET

Style sheets are an extremely important feature of Ventura Publisher. Ventura style sheets contain page settings, margin and column settings, and a series of typographic **tags**. These tags—as specified in the style sheet—can be applied to any paragraph in a chapter.

When a paragraph is marked with a tag, Ventura places an invisible marker in that paragraph, and the paragraph is formatted according to the text attributes associated with the paragraph tag it has been assigned. For example, suppose you set the body text (standard text paragraphs) of a style sheet to 9-point Helvetica (called Swiss in Ventura). All paragraphs marked with the Body Text tag would be formatted in 9-point Helvetica.

Using a style sheet, you can maintain design consistency throughout large documents. Furthermore, even if a number of word processors were used to create different parts of one document, when imported into the same style sheet, all text can appear the same in the final Ventura document. Even if the text has not been preformatted in the same manner, you can apply paragraph tags and text formatting features within Ventura to maintain design consistency. Another way Ventura style sheets help maintain design consistency is that as long as all people involved in producing a document use the same style sheet and paragraph tags, documents can always be produced consistent with previous versions.

Another major benefit of using style sheets is that you can instantly change the format of an entire chapter. By changing the settings of paragraph tags in a style sheet with the appropriate options under the Paragraph menu heading, you can change the look of an entire chapter in seconds. For example, you could change the previously mentioned 9-point Helvetica Body Text tag setting to 12-point Times Roman (called Dutch in Ventura), using the Font option under the Paragraph menu heading.

PLANNING YOUR DOCUMENT

Your first step is to revert to a paper and pencil. Sketch your basic, rough design. The more time you spend with the pencil and paper in the initial planning stages of creating a new Ventura style sheet, the quicker you will be able to create a new style sheet.

In Ventura's training guide, a Document Planning Form is provided, which is reproduced in Figure 8.1. You can make photocopies of this form and use them as part of your desktop publishing operation.

DOCUMENT PLANNING FORM

Document Name: ______________________________

Due Date: ______________________________

Text Files:

File Name:	Description:	W/Pkg:	Author:
________	________	________	________
________	________	________	________
________	________	________	________
________	________	________	________
________	________	________	________
________	________	________	________

Picture Files:

File Name:	Description:	Graphics Pkg:	Author:
________	________	________	________
________	________	________	________
________	________	________	________
________	________	________	________
________	________	________	________
________	________	________	________

Style Sheet:

Name: ______________________________

Modified to:(new name) ______________________________

Figure 8.1 Document Planning Form

Your first consideration is what the finished document will be. A newsletter's design should differ from that of a business report, and the designs of both will differ from that of a product brochure.

For each job, use the planning form in Figure 8.1 to organize your document and to identify which word processing documents will be imported into Ventura to make up the final document. This form can also be used to name the style sheet used and, if any alterations were made, to name the new style sheet.

UNDERSTANDING THE STYLE SHEET

The style sheet acts as a shell document and totally controls the format of your finished document. Style sheets contain paragraph tags, page settings, and frame settings.

Ventura style sheets use controls that are set in the Page, Frame, Paragraph, and Options menus. You can make settings in each of these menus to control the characteristics of each of your style sheets.

From the Page Menu, the following control settings can be used in creating a style sheet:

- Page Layout
- Widows and Orphans
- Auto-Numbering
- Footnote Settings

The Page Layout option affects all pages within the document. The Widows and Orphans and Auto-Numbering options affect all text within the document. Footnote settings affect text on the underlying page.

From the Frame menu heading, underlying page frames are controlled by settings assigned from the following options:

- Margins & Columns
- Sizing & Scaling
- Repeating Frame
- Vertical Rules
- Ruling Line Above
- Ruling Line Below
- Ruling Box Around
- Frame Background

From the Paragraph menu heading, settings for different tags are controlled by settings assigned from the following options:

- Font
- Alignment
- Spacing
- Breaks
- Tab Settings
- Special Effects
- Typographic Controls
- Ruling Line Above
- Ruling Line Below
- Ruling Box Around
- Assign Function Keys

Printer information can be set using options under the Options menu heading. Ventura lists typefaces, point sizes, and styles displayed in the Add/Remove Fonts dialog box, based on information stored in the current .WID file (the width table).

Forms for page layout and tag planning are provided in Ventura's training guide. These forms are rather limited and do not include spaces for all of the attributes you can assign in a style sheet. Appendix A contains a Style Sheet Control Form. Photocopy this form as many times as you need to create and maintain a record of individual style sheets. It is recommended that Style Sheet Control Forms be stored in a three-ring notebook near your work station for easy reference.

Because so many different attributes can be assigned to style sheets, the following sections will discuss their numerous settings. You can understand the discussion of these settings better by following the Style Sheet Control Form as you read. You will not need to use all the settings in these menus for each style sheet, but you have the option of using as many or as few as you want.

PAGE MENU SETTINGS

Several options available in the Page menu are stored in a style sheet and control the format of an entire chapter. Other options are stored by Ventura in a chapter file or perform a one-time-only function.

From the Page menu, information for the Page Layout, Widow & Orphans, Autonumbering, and Footnote Settings is recorded in the style sheet. Although you can also access the Headers & Footers, Turn Header On, Turn Footer On, Chapter Counter, and Page Counter options from the Page menu, these options are stored in the chapter file—not in the style sheet. (This convention allows you to use the style sheet for other documents with different headers, footers, and numbers.) You must set the Headers & Footers, Turn Header On, Turn Footer On, Chapter Counter, and Page Counter options from the Page menu each time you create a new chapter.

Other options available in the Page menu are Renumber Chapter, Re-Anchor Frames, Insert/Remove Page, and Go To Page. These functions change with each new situation and are not recorded in the style sheet or the chapter files.

Page Layout

To begin laying out your own style sheet, first select the Page menu, and then select the Page Layout option. The Page Layout dialog box appears.

First, select portrait or landscape orientation, depending on whether you want your pages to print 8.5" wide × 11" high or 11" wide × 8.5" high, respectively.

Next, select the paper type. You can choose from the following six options:

Half	8.5 inches by 5.5 inches
Letter	8.5 inches by 11 inches
Legal	8.5 inches by 14 inches
Double	11 inches by 17 inches
B5	17.6 centimeters x 15 centimeters
A4	21 x 29 centimeters

The next option is Sides. Selecting Single means that all pages will have exactly the same headers and footers, margins, column widths, vertical rules, and tag (i.e.,In From Left, In From Right) settings for both the left and right pages. Choose Double to allow different settings on left and right pages.

The next option is Start On. You can choose either Left Side or Right Side, which will determine if the first page of your chapter starts on the right or left side.

Tip: If you select Single Sides and Start on Left Side, only the Left Side settings for headers and footers, margins, column widths, vertical rules, and tag settings are applied to each page of the chapter. If you choose Single Side and Start on Right Side, only the right page will have the settings for headers & footers, margins, column widths, vertical rules, and tag settings applied. For most documents, you will want to use Double Sides.

The next option is **kerning**. Kerning is a method of space reduction used between specific letter pairs. The amount of space that would normally occur between those letters would look excessive because of the relationship between their shapes and the white space that surrounds them. Kerning conserves space, improves readability, and improves the overall design of your document. You can turn kerning on or off globally (i.e., throughout the entire document). As long as you are using PostScript fonts, you can use Kerning Globally On because PostScript fonts contain information enabling them to use kerning. If you are using fonts other than PostScript fonts, kerning may or may not be supported. Global kerning must be turned on at this point if you plan to use the Kerning option later in the Typographic Controls menu under the Paragraph menu heading.

After choosing the appropriate Kerning option, select OK.

Widows and Orphans

Select the Widows & Orphans option from the Page menu. The Widows & Orphans dialog box will appear.

A **widow** is a single line of text at the top of a page or column that has been separated from the paragraph on the previous page or previous column. An **orphan** is a single line of text at the bottom of a page or column that has been separated from a paragraph that begins on the next page or in the next column. The Widows & Orphans control will help your documents look better by eliminating widows and orphans.

Set the Minimum Isolated Lines number to whatever number of lines you prefer. The standard default setting is 2, which requires that a minimum of two lines must remain together or be forced to the next page or column, if possible.

When you have made your selection in the Widows & Orphans dialog box, select OK.

Auto-Numbering

Select the Auto-Numbering option from the Page menu. The Auto-Numbering dialog box will appear.

Auto-numbering will automatically insert section numbers before tagged paragraphs. These section numbers can contain any combination of styles and punctuation. This Ventura feature is particularly useful in reports and outlines.

To turn on Auto-Numbering, select On in the dialog box. Ten levels of Auto-Numbering are available. Position the cursor on Level 1. Then, choose which style of automatic number you prefer, such as 1,2 or A,B or I.,II. This choice will then place the words "tag name" on the Level 1 line. Use the backspace key to replace "tag name" with the name of the header to which you want to assign Auto-Numbering. For example, if you want Auto-Numbering assigned to headers, replace "tag name" with the actual paragraph tag name — "Header" in this example. Then, each time you use the Header paragraph tag in the chapter, Auto-Numbering will add the number style you assigned to Header. The numbers will appear in Body Text format unless you choose a different format, using the Text Attr option (discussed later) in the Auto-Numbering dialog box.

For example, suppose your Header paragraph tag has a Swiss 12-point italic font, and your Body Text tag has a Dutch 10-point font. If you choose the 1,2 (Arabic) numbering style for paragraphs tagged as "Header," and the fifth Header paragraph contains the words "All About Jollie Mollie," that header would appear as follows:

5

All About Jollie Mollie

Generated tags can also be assigned Auto-Numbering. Chapter numbers can also be assigned on any level.

There are two other selections on the Auto-Numbering dialog box: Suppress Previous Level and Text Attr. The Suppress Previous Level option is used when you do not want all previous levels of an outline to show on lower line levels. For example, in a typical outline, which resembles the following,

I.
    A.
    B.
        1.
        2.

on the third level, where the number 1 is located, you probably do not want previous levels—such as I.,A.,1—to be listed. You probably only want 1, as in the example, so select Suppress Previous Level to show only the level of the line.

Tip: When you select Suppress Previous Level, the code [-] is placed where your cursor is located. The minus sign in brackets [-] should be the first item on the line, so make sure your cursor is in the appropriate location when you select Suppress Previous Level.

The Text Attr. option adds special attributes to the text that makes up your Auto-Numbering. For example, if you want the Auto-Number-generated number to be in italics, select Text Attribute, and insert <I>, which is the code for turning on Italics. Type the tag name and then type <D>, which is the code for returning to normal text.

Auto-Numbering with Outlines

If you use an outline approach such as the typical outline of levels, I., A., 1., etc., you will not be able to reset the top level to any number other than I., which poses a real problem if you want to have more than one list with its own numbers in the same chapter.

There is a solution to this problem. Specify your first level as Body Text. Then establish your levels; your top level will now be level 2. If you do this, each time a paragraph with the tag Body Text is encountered, the Auto-Numbering function is reset. Each Body Text paragraph will be Auto-Numbered, which is probably not what you want. To eliminate Auto-Numbering from Body Text, simply press the Backspace key to delete the number. This technique will permit you to use as many Auto-Number outlines as you want within a chapter. When completed, your entry on Level 1 should be as follows:

Level 1: [*Body Text]

Inserting Text and Punctuation with Auto-Numbering

You can place text on any of the 10 different levels in the Auto-Numbering dialog box. Punctuation is also possible. To add a colon after the Header Number, for example, the Level line should be as follows:

Level x: [*Header 1,1]:

You can also insert text at the beginning of each paragraph. A good example of why you may want to use this trick is the familiar question-and-answer format. Suppose you want the name of the publication—in this example, "Today's Journal"—to appear at the beginning of each "Question" paragraph. The name of the paragraph tag is "Question." The entry on the level in the Auto-Numbering dialog box would be as follows.

Level x: [*Question]Today's Journal:

You can go one step further: if you want the text "Today's Journal:" to be in bold-italic, add the code <BI> . The entry should then be as follows:

Level x: [*Question] <BI>Today's Journal:

When you finish creating Auto-Numbering levels, select OK.

> **Tip:** In any Ventura dialog box, to erase an entire line entry, position the cursor on a line, and press the Esc key. This technique is faster than pressing Backspace or Delete to remove inserted text.

Footnotes

Select the Footnote Settings option from the Page menu. The Footnote Settings dialog box will appear.

The Footnote Settings option controls the format of footnotes placed in your chapters.

Under the Usage & Format option, there are four selections:

- **Off** disables the Footnote setting. One of the other three options must be selected to turn the Footnote setting on.

- **# From Start of Page (1,2,3)** restarts footnote numbering at the top of each page and automatically numbers each footnote with an Arabic number (1,2,3,etc.).

- **# From Start of Page (User-Defined)** restarts the footnote numbering at the top of each page, but instead of inserting Arabic numbers, it will insert whatever you enter in the User-Defined Strings section farther down in the dialog box.

- **# From Start of Chapter (1,2,3)** works the same way as # From the Start of Page (1,2,3) except that automatic numbering commences at the beginning of the chapter—not at the beginning of each page.

To change the setting to start on a footnote number other than one, position the cursor on the Start With # option, and set the new number you want.

The next option in the dialog box—the Number Template—permits you to place a text character directly before and after the footnote number. For example, an entry of (#) would position the footnote number between the parentheses. Other possible combinations include {#} , [#] , -#- , # , *#* , "#" , or :#: . The # character instructs Ventura where to place the footnote number.

The next option in the Footnote dialog box is Position of Number. You can choose No Shift, Superscript, or Subscript.

User-defined strings are used with the # From Start of Page (User-Defined) option. You can place any text string you need in these eight spaces.

Finally, you have the option of placing a line in the chapter to separate text from footnotes. Use the Separator Line Width, Space Above Line, and Height of Line settings to set the characteristics of the separator line.

When you finish with the footnote settings, select OK.

> **Tip:** You can turn footnotes off when using your style sheet. Turning off footnotes will not affect the text or settings stored in the style sheet.

FRAME MENU SETTINGS

Several settings available in Frame menu options are stored in a style sheet and therefore control the format of the underlying page frame.

Note: options discussed for your own style sheets deal only with the underlying page frame. Of course, you can access the Frame menu to assign attributes to other frames you later add to chapters, but for now, only the underlying page frame is discussed because its characteristics are stored in the style sheet. Changes made to any underlying page frame affect all underlying pages. Changes made to a frame placed on top of the underlying page frame using the Frame Setting function only affect that individual frame.

From the Frame menu, the Margins & Columns, Sizing & Scaling, Repeating Frame, Vertical Rules, Ruling Line Above, Ruling Line Below, Ruling Box Around, and Frame Background options are recorded in the style sheet. They are also used to create the format for the underlying page frame. Although you can access the Anchors & Captions, Table Counter, and Figure Counter options from the Frame menu, these options are stored in the chapter file—not in the style sheet.

Margins and Columns

Before selecting the Margins & Columns option in the Frame menu, be sure the Frame setting in the Function Selector box is activated and the underlying page is selected. (The Frame must cover the entire page.)

The first option in the Margins & Columns dialog box is # of columns. Select from one to eight columns. One column is used for layouts such as the one used for this book. Multiple columns are used for newspaper layouts, directory listings, newsletters, etc.

The number of columns selected will determine the number of columns automatically set for the entire document. You can always change the number of frames on an individual page by adding frames. Again, these added frames will be stored in the chapter file—not in the style sheet.

After selecting the number of columns, the next option is to apply the settings to the left or right page. In most cases, you will start with the right page; however, if you have chosen Start On Left Side in the Page Layout dialog box, you should start with the left page.

Next, type in the widths of your columns. Also, add the gutter width (white space between columns).

After entering column and gutter widths, enter the margin settnigs. These margins should not include space for headers or footers. Headers and footers are inserted in their own frames above and below the top and bottom margins.

Tip: If you are setting unequal column widths, enter the intended width of each column and the gutter widths; then check the Calculated Width line to be certain it equals (or is at least within) the Actual Frame Width. If necessary, make adjustments so the combination of your margins, column widths, and gutters equal the actual frame width.

If you are using double-sided pages (as indicated in the Page Layout dialog box), and if you want the right- and left-side settings to be different, you can then create the settings for the left page.

If you are using single-sided pages and do not want different settings, you can select Copy to Facing Page. This option produces a mirror image (i.e., reverses your settings) on the facing page, permitting a binding offset for your finished document.

If you do not want to copy Margins and Columns settings from one page to the other, switch pages on the Settings For line, and enter information for the other page.

When you have finished creating margin and column settings, select OK or press the Return key.

Ruling Lines

Both vertical and horizontal ruling lines can be applied to style sheets. These lines will be recorded in the style sheet and used in the underlying page frame, which permits them to be applied to every page in the chapter. Ruling lines set for any frame other than the underlying page frame are not recorded in the style sheet but in the chapter file.

Vertical Rules

The Vertical Rules option in the Frame menu permits you to place ruling lines between columns. You can set a vertical rule for either the left page, the right page, or both pages.

The first selection in the Vertical Rules Dialog box is Settings For: Left Page or Right Page. Choose a page to which you want to apply the vertical rule.

The next option is Inter. Col. Rules. This setting is for inter-column ruling lines, and if turned on, will automatically insert a vertical rule between columns, providing a newspaper-like appearance. If you use inter-column rules, you must also specify a width for thc vcrtical ruling line.

The next option is the Rule 1 Position. The vertical rule placement is measured from the left side of the page—not from the left side of the frame. You can position the rule within the underlying page frame. It need not be in the margin. After selecting the position of the vertical rule, you must specify the width of the rule.

You can add a second rule to the page by entering the information in the Rule 2 position.

The last selection is Inserts: Copy to Facing Page. If you selected Double-sided in the Page Layout dialog box and want the same ruling lines repeated on each page, select Copy to Facing Page. If you want different vertical rule settings for right and left pages, select the other page on the Settings For line, and enter the settings you want for that page.

Tip: If you place a frame, or text that has been tagged to be **frame wide**, across a vertical rule, the rule will be interrupted. Text that is tagged to be **column wide** will not interrupt the vertical rule or flow around it.

When all vertical rules have been set, select OK.

Ruling Lines Above and Below

As many as three ruling lines can be placed at the top or bottom of the underlying page by inserting the information in the underlying page frame. The three lines can be solid lines, dashes, or shaded patterns. Color can also be assigned to each ruling line. Each rule can have a different thickness, and the spacing between the lines can differ as well.

The widths of the ruling lines are automatically set equal to the width of the underlying page (i.e., the actual width of the paper).

Tip: Ruling lines above and below are independent of the frame's top and bottom margins (i.e., it is possible to position ruling lines so they fall across text).

The Ruling Box Around option in the Frame menu cannot be used in conjunction with the Ruling Line Above or the Ruling Line Below options.

Dialog Boxes for Ruling Lines Options

The dialog boxes for Ruling Lines Above, Ruling Lines Below, and Ruling Box Around are identical in appearance, so the dialog box will be discussed only once, but the same information applies to each of the three options.

Before selecting the Ruling Lines Above, Ruling Lines Below, or Ruling Box Around option in the Frame menu, activate the Frame setting in the Function Selector box and select the underlying page.

When the dialog box appears, the first option available is Width. The selections are None, Text, Margin, Column, Frame, or Custom. Choose Frame for this example.

The next option is Color. In most cases, you will want a black line; however, you can assign another color. (See Chapter 10 for more information about working with color in Ventura.)

The next option for the line is Pattern. Select Solid for a solid line, or select a number from one to seven to create a shaded ruling line. You can also make your ruling lines dashes. To do so, select Dashes Off, which—contrary to its name—turns dashes on.

There are three Space Above Rule and Height of Rule dimension categories in which to enter the thickness and height of your rule. As you enter the height and thickness of your rule, you will see an example of the rule inserted to the right side of the numbers. You can readjust the thickness of your rule by deleting and changing the numbers inserted in the dimension spaces.

If you choose to turn on the dash option, you can also set its width, spacing, a custom indent, or a custom width.

Tip: Note the measurement unit located below the dash dimension spaces. By moving the mouse cursor to the measurement units and clicking once, you can change the measurement units. The measurement units can be changed to inches, centimeters, picas, points, or fractional points.

For Ruling Lines Above, the distance between the first line and the top of your page is set in the Space Above Rule 1 selection in the dialog box. If you add a second line, enter the distance between the second line and the first line in the Space Below Rule 1 selection in the dialog box.

For Ruling Lines Below, the distance between the first line and the bottom of your text is set in the Space Above Rule 1 selection in the dialog box. If you add a second line, the Below Rule 1 setting becomes the distance between the first line and the second line. To create a third line, you must then enter the distance you want between the second and third lines in the Space Below Rule 2 selection in the dialog box.

If you don't want to add a second or third ruling line in the Ruling Lines Above or Ruling Lines Below options, be sure that 00 appears in those selection spaces.

Always be certain the overall spacing used by the Ruling Lines Above and Ruling Lines Below options does not exceed the height of the Top or Bottom Margin. If it does, your ruling lines will cover your text.

The Ruling Box Around option allows up to three lines to surround your text. As with the Ruling Lines Above and Below options, different thicknesses and different spacing can be assigned to each ruling box line.

The ruling box is placed by establishing a measurement for the distance between the box and the edge of the paper. The distance from the paper edge must be equal on all four sides. The ruling box, when selected and recorded in the style sheet, will appear in all of your chapter's pages.

Note: you cannot use Ruling Box Around option in conjunction with the Ruling Line Above and the Ruling Box Below features.

The selections for Ruling Box Around are the same as the Ruling Line Above and Ruling Line Below options. You can assign color, pattern, dashes, thickness, and spacing to the Ruling Box Around lines.

Determine the distance you want between the edges of the page and the ruling box. Enter that distance in the Space Above Rule 1 selection space. If you will be using more than one box, the Space Below Rule 1 option is where you enter the amount of space you want between the first, or outside, line in the first ruling box and the line that makes up the second box.

If you decide not to add a second or third box within the first box, make sure 00 appears in the second and third line selection spaces.

Always make sure the overall space used in the Ruling Box Around option does not exceed the size of margins set for the text. If it does, the ruling lines will cover your text.

When you finish entering selections in the Ruling Lines Above, Ruling Lines Below, or Ruling Box Around dialog box, select OK. You will be able to see your rules on the underlying page frame. If the appearance is not what you wanted or expected, simply enter the Frame mode, select the appropriate option from the Frame menu, and make your changes.

Frame Background

For the underlying page frame of most documents, you will use the Hollow setting in the Frame Background dialog box because it places your document on a plain white background; however, if you ever do need a different background, use the same dialog box to set it.

Before selecting the Frame Background option in the Frame menu, be sure the Frame setting in the Function Selector box above the side bar is activated and that the underlying page frame is selected (click the mouse button within the frame).

When the Frame Background dialog box appears, the first option is Color (see Chapter 10 for more information). Select a color for your frame background.

The second option is Pattern. Click the mouse on one of the seven numbers; you will see the pattern it creates in the result box.

> **Tip:** Selecting a dark background will often make your text difficult or even impossible to read. For most documents, choose lighter patterns.

When you finish setting the color and pattern of your frame background, select OK.

PARAGRAPH MENU SETTINGS

Paragraph tags are stored in the style sheet. You must assign a tag for each different paragraph format in your chapter. Ventura permits up to 128 different tags per style sheet.

Most options available in the Paragraph menu settings are stored in a style sheet, and are used to control the format of the paragraph tags. You can select the following options: Font, Alignment, Spacing, Breaks, Tabs, Settings, Special Effects, Typographic Controls, Ruling Line Above, Ruling Line Below, Ruling Box Around, and Assign Function Keys. Although 10 different options can be assigned to your tags, in most cases, you will only be using three: Font, Alignment, and Spacing.

Note: you must first load a text file and highlight a paragraph to be tagged before you make any changes in paragraph tags. Being required to first tag a paragraph permits you to see how the text appears as you change options. It is recommended that you load a previously unused text file for setting and creating style sheets unless you don't mind changing tags previously assigned to that text.

Before you can choose options in the Paragraph menu, you must enter the Paragraph mode by selecting the Paragraph Tagging function in the Function Selector box above the side bar or by pressing the Ctrl/I key combination.

The best place to start creating your own tag attributes is with the Body Text tag. A tag for Body Text must be in each style sheet because Ventura has reserved a tag for body text, and you cannot remove it. You can, however, change the characteristics of body text.

> **Tip:** To change the format of a word or section of text within a paragraph, use the Text Editing function labeled "Text" in the Function Selector box above the side bar. Any changes made with the Text Editing function take priority over paragraph tags.

Later in this chapter, you will learn how to change, add, and delete paragraph tags. Now, the available tagging characteristics will be discussed. Remember that a paragraph must first be highlighted in Paragraph mode before you can access the various options in the Paragraph menu.

Naming Paragraph Tags

Ventura permits up to 128 different tags per style sheet; however, well-designed documents generally use only a few tags. Design experts recommend that only one or two typefaces and a few point sizes be used in a single document. Avoid the temptation to use too much bold or italic type. If you use too many distinctive features, none of your text will stand out. To emphasize everything is to emphasize nothing.

When naming tags, use short, descriptive names. Shorter tag names make it easier to preformat text with a word processor.

Develop your own standards for tag names. For example, if you have a tag named "Byline," maintain consistent attributes in your style sheets (e.g., always centered, always in italics, always in 12-point Helvetica). If you use more than one type of byline, use a different name for each type; simply number them (Byline1, Byline2, etc.) or use descriptive abbreviations (Byline 12pt, Byline 14pt). You can choose any settings you want, but consistency helps prevent confusion.

It is also good practice to store a copy of each of your style sheets on a floppy disk. You can also keep a list of each tag and its attributes as a reference.

Keeping related tags alphabetically similar is helpful because Ventura automatically alphabetizes tag names in the side bar in the upper left corner of your screen. For example, Head1, Head2, and Head3 would be better tag names than Heading, Subhead1, Subhead2 because the Head1, Head2, Head3 tag names will be displayed together in the side bar.

Tip: Never use only uppercase letters for tag names. Instead, use a combination of upper- and lowercase. Tags placed during preformatting that do not match tag names available in the current side bar are displayed in uppercase. Such text will be assigned the same attributes as body text. The only way you can recognize these misplaced tags is to not use only uppercase letters for your tag names. If a mismatch of tag names does occur, select Load. Diff. Style from the File menu and choose another style sheet (the current one may not be the correct one), or modify the attributes of tags appearing in uppercase. If you change the attributes of tags appearing in uppercase, remember to use the Rename Tag option under the Paragraph menu heading to convert the uppercase tag name to mixed case or lowercase.

Generated Tags

Whenever you create a header, footer, caption, automatic number, table of contents, or index, Ventura automatically creates a **generated tag**. These tags—identified as Z_HEADER, Z_FOOTER, Z_INDEX, etc.—use the same text attributes that exist for body text. You can change text attributes for generated tags. For example, you may want the same font size in the header, but you may want bold rather than normal type. Assign those attributes to the generated tag by first choosing the Paragraph mode in the Function Selector box. Then, select the text assigned to that generated tag (for example, the footer), and then use the Paragraph menu options to change the attributes.

Generated tags always begin with an uppercase Z. These tags are normally not displayed in the side bar, but you can display them by changing the setting in the Set Preferences option to Show Generated Tags.

Ventura's 128-tag limit includes generated tags.

Font

The Font option permits you to choose the typeface, type size, type style, and color for each paragraph.

Select the Font option under the Paragraph menu heading. When the Font dialog box appears, select the type style by choosing one of the Face options. (The type style or faces available will be determined by what printer and fonts you have installed.)

Next, choose the type size. If you are using a PostScript printer, select the point size in the Custom Size option in the PostScript area of the Font dialog box. Any size between 1 and 254 points is permitted.

For other printers, more limited font sizes are available. If you are restricted in point size because of your printer, choose one of the predetermined font sizes in the Size box.

You should then choose the type style and color. When you have finished, select OK. The tagged paragraph will appear with your changes. You can return to the Font dialog box and make any additional changes.

Alignment

Alignment settings control the appearance of your text in columns or frames. These settings control the horizontal appearance of your text. After you select Alignment in the Paragraph menu, the Alignment dialog box appears.

The first choice is Alignment, and there are four options: Left, Center, Right, and Justified.

The second choice is Hyphenation. You can turn hyphenation off or use the USENGLISH dictionary for automatic hyphenation of your text.

The third choice is Successive Hyphens. You can choose from one to five or unlimited succesive lines for hyphenation. This setting controls how many rows of text you will allow Ventura to hyphenate in a row. A setting of 3 only permits three successive rows of text to be hyphenated.

Overall width is the fourth choice in the Alignment dialog box. You can select Column-Wide or Frame-Wide. If you choose Column-Wide, your text will be inserted only into the column. If you choose Frame-Wide, the text will extend through and across all columns to the right and left margins.

Tip: Use the Frame-Wide selection for chapter titles and other headings if you want the text to extend across the page.

The fifth choice is First Line, where you can choose Indent or Outdent settings. This feature permits you to force the first line of text in or out from the rest of the paragraph. The location of that first line is determined by the setting (in inches) in the In/Outdent width box. You can also choose to indent or outdent more than one line by indicating how many lines you want in the In/Outdent Height box.

The final option is Relative Indent. If you choose a relative indent, the next paragraph starts on the next line in the position where the last paragraph stopped, as in the following example:

When you choose a relative indent, the next paragraph begins where the first one left off.

This is an example.

Note: you cannot use the Indent option with right-aligned or centered text.

When you finish with your alignment choices, select OK.

Spacing

The Spacing option in the Paragraph menu determines the space between lines and paragraphs. It can also be used to set temporary margins. When the Spacing dialog box appears, the first options available are Above, Below, Inter-Line, and Inter-Paragraph. Insert your choices in the spaces.

The Above and Below options add space between two differently tagged paragraphs. Inter-Paragraph adds space between paragraphs with the same tag. For many documents, you will probably set the Inter-Paragraph space to 0. The Above and Below settings will hold your preferences for space between paragraphs.

Inter-Line spacing determines the space between each line of text. This setting is very important because if you have too much space, the text will be hard to read, and if you have too little space between lines, ascenders and descenders of your typefaces will overlap. Make sure you have correctly chosen the Inter-Line Spacing. Space between lines is called **leading**. The term originated when printers used metal type and placed various-width pieces of lead between moveable type.

The rule of thumb is to use leading at least equal to the height of the typeface. In other words, 10-point type requires at least 10-point leading. Often, however, one or two points are added to the leading to make text easier to read. To avoid that compressed look, place 12-point leading between lines of 10-point text. You should consider adding even more space between lines if you are using extremely wide columns.

The next option is Add In Above. You can choose Always or When Not At Column Top. If you choose When Not At Column Top, any additional space above the paragraph will not be used when the tagged paragraph is at the top of a page or column. The Always option will always insert the space specified in Add In Above.

Settings For is the next option. You can apply different settings to right and left pages. Choose the page where the spacing will apply.

In From Left and In From Right are the next two options. These settings permit temporary margins. The In From Left and In From Right settings can be different for right- and left-side pages.

Tip: Use the In From Left setting to indent an entire paragraph. You can use this option instead of using the Indent option in the Alignment dialog box.

Multiple-Column Spacing

If you are creating a style sheet with multiple columns, it is important to consider multiple-column spacing. You will want the columns of text to be aligned. To be sure they align, the sum of the Inter-Line Space, Inter-Paragraph space, the Above space or Below Space, and the width of the ruling lines should be whole numbers such as 1, 2, 3, 4, etc. It is highly recommend that you use this formula when considering spacing in a multiple-column format.

The final option is Copy to Facing Page. This option only copies the setting from the In From Left or In From Right option to the facing page.

When you have made your choices in the Spacing dialog box, select OK.

Breaks

The Breaks option controls forced interruptions in text paragraphs. In the Break dialog box, you can create three types of Breaks: Page, Column, or Line.

The Page Break option determines whether a paragraph will always start or end a page. You can also choose Before/Until Left or Before/Until Right, which will only permit a paragraph to start on the left or right page. If one of these options is used, Ventura will automatically insert a blank page so your tagged paragraph will only start on the left or right page.

Tip: Because Ventura ignores page breaks inserted in text by a word processor, the Page Break option can be important. For example, for a book chapter tag, selecting Before in the Page Break option allows each new chapter to start on its own page.

The Column Break option determines if a paragraph will always begin or end a column.

The Line Break option determines whether a paragraph can begin on the same line as the previous paragraph or end on the same line as the next paragraph.

The Next Y Position option is used to decide if the next paragraph can begin on the same line as the last line of your paragraph. If you choose Beside Last Line of Prev. Para., and if no break is set between two paragraphs, the second paragraph begins on the same line in which the first paragraph ends. In most cases, leave Next Y Position set to Normal.

The Keep With Next option places two paragraphs together on the same page. It forces Ventura to keep the next paragraph with the one being tagged.

Tip: Ventura's Keeping With Next option is a powerful tool that is often overlooked by users. This feature should always be used with Headline or Title tags because it will prevent a headline or title from being left alone on the bottom of a page.

The standard or default settings for the Break option that will be used for most non-headline tags are as follows:

Page Break:	**No**
Column Break:	**No**
Line Break:	**Before**
Next Y Position:	**Normal**
Allow Within:	**Yes**
Keep With Text:	**No**

The standard or default settings of the Break option that will be used for most headline or main section tags are as follows:

Page Break:	**No**
Column Break:	**No**
Line Break:	**Before**
Next Y Position:	**Normal**
Allow Within:	**Yes**
Keep With Text:	**Yes**

After you have chosen break preference, select OK.

Tab Settings

Ventura's tabs are used for alignment of text or columns. Tabs in Ventura work just as they do in your word processor. Tabs become more important in Ventura, in which you often use proportionally spaced text (text in which each character occupies a different predetermined width). You cannot use spaces to align tables or listings when using proportional text; you must use tabs.

Whenever Ventura encounters a horizontal tab, it positions the character that follows the tab on the next tab location. A total of 16 tab locations is permitted in a paragraph.

When the Tab dialog box appears, you must first select the tab number you want to set. Next, choose whether the text to be positioned on the tab is to be left-, center-, right-, or decimal-aligned.

The next option, Tab Display, offers two choices: Shown as Open Space or Shown as Leader Char. If you choose Shown as Open Space, open space will be shown between tabs.

If you want a Leader Character, select Shown as Leader Char. Then, move to the Leader Char: selection and choose spaces, ... (ellipses), ____ (underline), or Other. If you choose Other, you can check Appendix E of Ventura's reference guide to find the decimal number that corresponds to the character you want placed in the tab space.

The Leader Spacing option is where you indicate the amount of space you want between the leader characters.

> **Tip:** Do not use tabs to indent your first line of text. Use the Indent option in the Alignment dialog box.

You must select tab locations. Expressed in inches, the measurement is always from the left edge of the column.

When you finish setting your tabs, select OK.

Special Effects

The Special Effects option in the Paragraph menu allows you to add bullets or a Big First Character (called a dropped capital) at the beginning of a paragraph. The font used for the Bullet or Big First Character can be different from the font used for the rest of the paragraph.

Big First Char

If you choose Big First Char, click in the Set Font Properties box. You will see the familiar Font menu. Here, you can select the Face, Style, Size, Color, and Character Shift (in most cases, Zero shift will provide the best appearance) options you want, and then select OK to return to the Special Effects Dialog box.

The Space for Big First Char section instructs Ventura as to how many lines of text the first character will occupy. When you select Normal, Ventura automatically chooses how many lines the first character will occupy, based on the options you choose in the Set Font Properties dialog box. Selecting Custom permits you to tell Ventura how many lines you want the First Big Character to occupy.

For example, if you want some paragraphs to begin with a dropped capital that occupies two lines of text, enter Paragraph mode (Ctrl/I) and highlight a paragraph. For this example, name your tag BigFirst, using the Add New Tag option above the side bar; then choose the Special Effects option under the Paragraph menu heading. Choose Big First Char, and then click on the Set Font Properties box. For this example, choose Dutch 18-point bold in the Font dialog box that appears. Next, choose Custom in the Space for Big Char section, and set number of lines to 2. If the rest of your text is 10-point Dutch, a paragraph tagged as BigFirst will resemble the following:

This is an example of how the Space for Big Char option can be used.

Bullet

If you choose Bullet, you can use a larger or smaller font for the bullet than for the rest of the text, using the Font Settings For Bullet option.

Select the Show Bullet As option to choose which character you want as your bullet. To use other options than those available, select Other and place the text cursor on the Bullet Char line. Then, type the ASCII number of the character. You can use the table in Appendix E in your Ventura reference guide to find the number of the character you want for your bullets.

For this example, choose 14-point Dutch, and choose the first bullet option in the dialog box (ASCII number 195).

Select the Indent After Bullet option, and specify the space between the bullet and the text that will follow it. For this example, specify .15 inches.

> **Tip:** If you are using bullets, you must use the Indent After Bullet option. If you do not indent after the bullet, text from the first line will be written over the bullet.

When you finish making selections in the Special Effects dialog box, select OK.

A bulleted paragraph with the selections you just made should resemble the following:

●This is an example of the Bullet Special Effects option.

Typographic Controls

The Typographic Controls option in the Paragraph menu permits you to control kerning, letter spacing, and tracking. It also controls the placement of underlines in your text and the use of overscore and strike-through.

When the Typographic Controls dialog box appears, it may first seem overwhelming, but like all Ventura dialog boxes, it can easily be used.

The first selection is Automatic Kerning. For the tagged paragraph, Automatic Kerning can be turned on or off. To view differences in kerning on your screen, make sure On-Screen Kerning is turned on in the Options Menu.

Kerning will slow text formatting. The information in your font width table for the printer must also include kerning information for the Kerning option to work. PostScript fonts supplied with Ventura include this information; fonts for other printers do not. Automatic Kerning can also be turned off for all tags by selecting Globally Off in the Page Layout Option.

The next selection in the Typographic Controls dialog box is Letter Spacing. As each paragraph is automatically justified by Ventura, the words are positioned evenly on each line of text. When Ventura finds there is not enough space without disobeying the Minimum Space Width, it will then insert the last word on the next line. If the word is long compared to the length of the line (this will usually occur in multi-column chapters), the space between words could be too much, creating what is called a **loose line**.

If letter spacing is turned on, additional space is added between letters until the space between words is less than the maximum space width.

To use the Letter Spacing option, turn it on and set the Minimum Space Width setting to less than the Normal Space Width setting. A typical minimum space width is in the range of 0.500 to 0.750 (50% to 75% of the Normal Space Width). Maintain the Normal Space Width of 1.000. Set the Maximum Space Width to the largest space between words permitted during Ventura's justification process. A typical number is 2.000, which is double the normal space width. These measurements are made in **ems**, a typographical term referring to the width of an uppercase M.

The Normal Space Width setting permits you to specify the amount of space you want between each word. This option lets you change the size of your paragraphs by adding or deleting space between words. For example, if you change the Normal Space Width setting to 1.500, you would place one and one-half ems between each word instead of just one em.

Because ems vary from font to font, there is no standard measurement for space between words. Experiment with the Normal Space Width, but always start with 1.000 as the Standard Width Space setting.

Adding space between words is only important if you are using justification. It becomes more critical if you use narrow columns because fewer words can be placed on each text line.

Tip: You can show loose lines by accessing the Options menu and selecting the Show Loose Lines option. Doing so will highlight loose lines in your text. You can make corrections then to your lines by editing, changing the controls described in this chapter, or manually adding spaces or hyphenation.

The next option available in the Typographic Controls menu is Tracking. This option is used to increase or decrease space between characters. You can select Looser or Tighter; then, you must enter on the Tracking line the amount you want Ventura to increase or decrease space between characters.

The remaining options—Overscore Height, Strike-through Height, Underline 1 Height, and Underline 2 Height—permit you to customize the height of each line and the amount of space each line should be shifted.

Tip: Change the height of these line attributes each time you change the font size. For example, if you change from 18- to 9-point type, these line attributes must be cut in half.

Underline 1 controls the height and shift for a single underline or the top line of a double underline. Underline 2 controls the height and shift for the bottom line in a double underline.

When you finish making your choices in the Typographic Controls dialog box, select OK.

Ruling Line Above, Ruling Line Below, and Ruling Box Around

Just as you can place a ruling line above or below—or a box around—a frame, you can also place a ruling line above or below a paragraph. You can also place a box around a paragraph.

The Ruling Lines dialog box in the Paragraph menu is the same as the Ruling Lines dialog boxes in the Frame menu. Accordingly, for specific information about the settings, refer to the Ruling Lines Above and Below section earlier in this chapter.

Tip: Do not use the Ruling Box Around option for columns of text. If you do, you will find a Ruling Box placed around the first section of text; however, if the text is carried onto the next page or into another column, the next section will not be enclosed in a box. Use Ruling Box Around for only short paragraphs or section headings.

After you select the settings for your Ruling Line Above, Ruling Line Below, or Ruling Box Around, select OK.

Using Function Keys for Your Tags

The Assign Func. Keys menu permits you to use function keys to assign frequently used tags to paragraphs in your style sheets. This menu prevents you from switching between Paragraph and Text modes when editing text. While editing, if you want to tag a paragraph, simply place the cursor in the paragraph you want to tag (in Text or Paragraph mode) and press the function key assigned to the tag you want to use.

To access the Assign Func. Keys menu, press the Ctrl/K key combination or select it under the Paragraph menu heading while in Paragraph mode. Function keys F1-F10 are listed in the menu. Simply type in the name of the tag you want to assign to each function key.

If you type a tag name that does not exist in your style sheet, an error message will appear on your screen. After pressing the Return key or clicking on OK, you can return to the Assign Func. Keys option. A blank line will appear where you entered the name of the tag that does not exist. Then, simply reenter the correct name of the tag. If you enter the tag twice, only the first entry will be used.

When you finish assigning function keys, select OK.

After assigning function keys, you can use them whether you are in the Paragraph or Text modes. When you press a function key, the tag assigned to that function key will be assigned to the selected paragraph or the paragraph containing the text cursor. The real power of this feature is that while editing text, you can change the tag without changing from Text to Paragraph modes.

Tip: Style sheets included with Ventura reserve the F10 kcy for Body Text. You can assign a different function key for Body Text, but remember, just as Ventura requires you to have a Body Text paragraph tag, it also requires you to have a Body Text function key, so you cannot remove Body Text from the Assign Func. Keys dialog box entirely. Being able to quickly revert to Body Text if you accidentally assign the wrong tag to a paragraph is useful. Consistency of function key assignments from style sheet to style sheet is a good idea, so you may want to retain the F10 key Body Text assignment in your own style sheets.

Again, standardization always helps you work faster with Ventura. Develop your own function key conventions (e.g., the Byline tag should always be F3).

OPTIONS MENU

Within the Options Menu, the Set Printer Info. option is available when you create style sheets. The printer width table—identified with the extension .WID—can be changed but only if you plan to use different printers. Ventura must know the width of your characters to properly adjust the spacing of words and characters. The information Ventura needs to perform this spacing is stored in the width tables. If you want to use a printer width table other than the one shown in the Set Printer Info. dialog box, enter the new name. When finished, select OK.

USING AND MODIFYING VENTURA'S STYLE SHEETS

Often, you will be able to use one of the 25 style sheets included with Ventura. You can create your own style sheets by adding new paragraph tags and making other modifications to these style sheets. When you make significant modifications, be sure to save the style sheet under a new name. Style sheet modifications are saved whenever the current chapter is saved. If you do not want these changes to affect other documents that use the same style sheet, you must select the Save As New Style option under the File menu heading and enter a different style sheet name *before* you save your chapter. If you save it under its original name, the attributes of the original style sheet will be permanently altered; however, if you inadvertently modify any of the 25 original style sheets supplied with Ventura, you can delete the modified style sheets from the TYPESET subdirectory and re-copy the original style sheets from the Ventura Examples Disk #2.

If the standard style sheets suit your needs, use them. You can refer to Appendix L in the Ventura reference guide for information concerning each style sheet's attributes.

You can modify the existing tags of a style sheet by first entering paragraph mode (press the Ctrl/I key combination) and then selecting the tag you want to change. Next, assign the tag to a paragraph, and, under the Paragraph menu heading, select the option you want to modify, making the appropriate changes. For example, you can change the font size and typeface, inter-line spacing, tabs, and alignment (e.g., flush-left, centered, justified, etc.) associated with a particular paragraph tag using the Font, Spacing, Tab Settings, and Alignment options, respectively. When selected, each option listed under the Paragraph menu heading produces an appropriate dialog box for modifying that aspect of a paragraph tag.

Once you have entered your changes and approved them by pressing the Return key or clicking OK, you can see the results immediately in the selected paragraph. If you like your changes, keep them. If not, revise them now because all paragraphs assigned that tag will be affected by them.

You can also create new tags. To do so, you must enter Paragraph mode. Highlight a paragraph with a tag whose attributes you want to copy. (Any tag will do because to create new tags, you simply modify existing ones.) Then, select the Add New Tag option above the side bar on the left side of the screen. A dialog box appears. You must enter a name for your new tag before assigning its characteristics. The name of the tag you have chosen to copy from appears at the bottom of the dialog box. After you click OK or press the Return key, the name of your new tag appears in the dialog box. Then, you can simply modify the characteristics copied from the previous tag.

You can erase any tags you no longer want by entering the Paragraph mode and assigning to a paragraph the tag you want to remove. Select the Remove Tag option under the Paragraph menu heading. The name of the tag you want to delete will appear in the Remove Tag dialog box. Enter the name of the tag to which you want to convert the highlighted text. The default is Body Text. Note that the Body Text tag is the only tag that must appear in all style sheets. You can modify its characteristics, but you cannot remove it.

Building New Style Sheets

As you continue to expand your knowledge and use of Ventura, you will certainly want to create your own designs and style sheets. The style sheet controls the underlying, or master, page frame and, therefore, the basic design of pages in a document. Frames added after a style sheet is selected are not affected by the attributes assigned to the style sheet itself. Only the master page frame is affected by the style sheets.

After you have an initial plan, the fastest way to begin building your own style sheet is to load the style sheet called DEFAULT.STY, using the Load Different Style option under the File menu heading. DEFAULT.STY is a simple style sheet that contains only one tag, Body Text. It also contains settings for basic items such as margins. This style sheet is located on Disk #2 in the Ventura software package. When you first install Ventura on your hard drive, this style sheet, along with the others, is automatically copied into the TYPESET subdirectory. Ventura always uses the file extension .STY to identify a style sheet, and you should use it when naming style sheets of your own.

The next step is to load a text file. This is sample text that can be formatted as you make changes in your new style sheet. If the text you load was saved with a style sheet other than DEFAULT.STY, simply select the Load Different Style option under the File menu heading and load DEFAULT.STY.

When building new style sheets, use the following steps:

1. **Change the Margins and the Columns**. From the Frame menu, select the Margins and Columns option. Set the margin size to whatever is appropriate for your document.

> **Tip:** In the Margins and Columns menu, if settings for only one page are defined, Ventura automatically makes the right- and left-side pages identical. If your finished document is to be bound, you should add space for the inside margins to allow the space for either drilling holes or stapling and binding. For this sort of finished document, add more margin space to the right on left-side pages and more margin space to the left on right-side pages.

2. **Select the Page menu.** Change the Page Layout to your new settings. You should also set the Widow and Orphan control from the Page Menu. And you should set Auto-Numbering and Footnote settings.

3. **Select the Frame menu**. Choose the Vertical Rules, and establish your settings.

4. **Create New Tags** by first clicking on the Paragraph Tagging function. Then, select the Add New Tag button located just below the Function Selector on the left side of your screen. Name the new tag, and click OK. When you click OK, the new tag will become part of the list in the side bar. The new tag is automatically assigned to the selected text.

5. **Repeat step 4** to add additional tags.

6. **Save the new Style Sheet** by selecting the File menu. Choose Save As New Style.

KEEPING TRACK OF YOUR CUSTOMIZED STYLE SHEETS

As you now realize, Ventura style sheets contain a great deal of information about the format of chapters.

Plan now to keep track of your style sheets. Use the Style Sheet Control Form provided in Appendix A, and, in a notebook or special folder, keep a sample of any document you create. Use your samples to develop new style sheets.

The power of Ventura style sheets can be overwhelming. If you have a problem making a format appear exactly as you want, the answer can often be found in the style sheet. To become truly proficient at using Ventura, you must learn to master style sheets. Recording your settings on the Style Sheet Control Form and keeping a sample document for future reference will help you keep track of which style sheets produce what effects and how they produce them.

CHAPTER 9

WORKING WITH COMMERCIAL PRINTERS

Unlike other desktop publishing books, this book discusses working with a printer to mass-produce finished Ventura documents. Mass-production is the last step before distribution. A printer (i.e., the person or company with a printing press) will use your camera-ready document for mass-production. Small quantities of documents—usually 50 or less—can be printed on a photocopier.

In most other cases, a printer takes a photograph of your original, camera-ready Ventura document and makes a **plate**. (For large runs, this is a metal plate; for short runs—100 or less copies—most printers use a paper plate. Other printers use plastic plates.) Metal plates are usually coated with a chemical that reacts to light. During the plate-making process, light is directed to the film. In effect, this is much like taking a picture; the sensitive material on the plate serves as film. The image area on the plate attracts ink and repels water, and the non-image background area repels ink and attracts water, which is the principal of offset printing.

The printer will only perform one process: printing the document. The printer will not be setting type, performing traditional paste-up, or submitting proofs. The printer's page-composition services have been replaced by Ventura.

In the past few years, a new form of printing business has arrived—quick printing franchises. They stress service, offer competitive prices, and should not be overlooked. They are limited in completing large jobs; they prefer smaller jobs. Other large commercial printers would rather have large jobs and will quote exhorbitant prices for small jobs, hoping you will take your work elsewhere.

WORKING WITH A PRINTER

Even if you have an exceptional working relationship with one or more printers, keep them competitive by seeking other quotes.

Lowest price should not be the sole criteria for choosing a printer; your printer must deliver a good product and outstanding service. Make sure your printer can do the assigned job. For example, not all print shops have large web presses that can print newspapers. Many cannot perform thermography, and others cannot print a job on 11" × 17" paper.

One of the first points to consider is paper. Thousands of different types of papers are manufactured for printing. Paper prices and qualities vary tremendously. Your printer should provide you with free paper samples. Carefully choose your paper; the price of paper is a major portion of the printing cost. Paper quality also affects the quality of the finished product.

There are many types of white paper—bright white, off-white, etc. Paper comes in different weights (16-lb., 20-lb., 24-lb., etc.) and coatings (flat, glossy, semi-gloss, matte, etc.). Papers include additives from the manufacturing process. Bleaches, starches, fillers, and other chemicals are added to papers to create different characteristics.

It is important how paper handles ink when applied. Coated papers are often used to help ink stay on the paper and not be absorbed into the fibers. Your printer should help you with paper selection. Many printers also provide sample charts of available ink colors.

Printers also provide many other services, including hole punching, saddle stitching, stapling, folding, collating, padding, binding, and die cutting. Some printers will pick up camera-ready copy and deliver finished jobs.

It is important that you develop a good working relationship with a printer (or two). You should be able to see the type of equipment the printer is using, actual samples of print jobs being produced, and the environment in which your document will be printed.

Sheet-fed vs. Web Printing Presses

Two types of printing presses are most often used. **Sheet-fed** printing presses print on one pre-cut piece of paper at a time. **Web** presses use a large roll of paper that is fed through the printing press. Several pages are printed across the width of the paper; after printing, the pages are folded and cut. This arrangement of printed pages on the large sheet (the layout) is called an **imposition**. (Newspapers are printed on a web press, as are magazines and many books.) When the printed paper is folded and cut, the new pages are referred to as **signatures**. After cutting, signatures are bound. Many books have smaller signatures bound into one larger signature.

Web presses print at high speeds and are therefore only used for large runs. A web press can print tens of thousands of 64-page newspapers per hour. For small jobs, such as 1000 11" × 17" pages or envelopes, the sheet-fed press is most often used. Sheet-fed presses are also used when exact color reproduction is required. Tight color registration is not easily achieved on a web press.

Web presses use large paper sizes, and it is not practical to use a web press for small jobs. By the time the web press achieves its regular running speed, the small quantity would have already been printed. Of course, if you have a job that can or should be printed on a web press, it is less expensive than printing on a sheet-fed press.

Saving Money on Print Jobs

Following are suggestions for reducing printing costs:

1. **Always seek competitive bids.** Printers are notorious for overbidding jobs, and prices vary as much as 100% from one shop to the next. Never give work to a printer without checking at least one other printer for a more competitive price.

2. **Never give work to a printer without first requesting an estimate or actual price for your print job.** Any reputable printer will be happy to provide a written price quote.

3. **Use standard ink colors.** Some jobs might require a flaming chartreuse, but the printer must mix special colors from an assortment of inks, and there will be a charge for that service. For most jobs, standard ink colors are fine, and they are cheaper.

4. **Select the right paper.** Always specify what kind of paper you want for a particular job. Don't let the printer choose your paper. Newsprint will look terrible for a corporate report. Also, colored inks require a coated surface. Buy paper with proper weight and finish for your jobs.

5. **Consider using colored paper.** Black ink on colored paper creates a two-color job that costs less than two colors on white paper. Similarly, two colors on colored paper creates a more economical three-color job.

6. **Use the two-up method of printing when possible.** For example, assume you have two forms, and both are to be printed on 8.5" × 11" paper. Order the same quantity of both forms, and ask the printer to run them through a press capable of printing on 11" × 17" paper. When finished, the printer can cut the 11" × 17" paper in half. This technique should always save you money and is exactly what many printers do to save their own money and time. Use the same method—if your printer has a big enough printing press—to print your materials four-up (17" × 22").

7. **Use standard-size paper whenever possible.** Printers buy paper in standard sizes, and when you deviate from a standard size, it always costs more. For example, if you want a 9" × 11" form, you are paying for 11" × 17" paper *and* an extra charge for paper cutting.

8. **Print on both sides of the paper whenever possible.** It costs less to print a 20-page report on both sides of 10 pages than it does to print 20 one-sided pages.

9. **Check the attitude of your printer when you supply camera-ready copy.** Remember, you are eliminating a service the printer would like to do for you (at an additional cost, of course). Ask what a job would cost if the printer typeset and printed it. There should be a substantial difference between the cost of a typesetting and printing a job as opposed to printing camera-ready copy. Make sure your printer is not penalizing you by increasing printing costs when you supply camera-ready copy.

10. **Order sufficient quantities of your job.** It is better to have too many than too few of the brochures, newsletters, etc. that your job requires, but order as close to the exact amount needed as possible so you won't be throwing away money on every job.

11. **Solicit the printer's opinion.** Printers are experts at the actual printing process. Always ask, "Is there a better way?"

Other Considerations

If you are using a laser printer as your final output device, consider asking the printer to reduce the final image by 10% or 20%. Reducing final images from the laser printer makes lower resolution far less apparent.

The standard paper size for a laser printer is 8.5" × 11". In the Page Layout option in Ventura's Page menu, you can select a paper size larger than 8.5" × 11". During printing, Ventura will present a special dialog box asking what action should be taken to fit this oversized page on 8.5" × 11" paper. If you are using a PostScript printer, you can choose to shrink the page. You can also choose to overlap, which produces multiple pages that can be pasted together. Select this option for oversized pages.

Use crop marks to help your printer trim and align pages as necessary. Remember, the printer trims these marks off paper, so you can use them only when the size of the finished page is less than the size of the paper produced by your laser printer. For example, if you place crop marks on an 8.5" × 11" inch page, the finished page will be 7" × 9" or smaller. (The size of crop marks is set in the Sizing & Scaling dialog box when working in the underlying page frame.) To place crop marks on a page so the finished, trimmed paper will be 8.5" × 11", choose legal paper size in the Page Layout menu, and choose overlap when printing.

Use special laser printer paper. All papers are not equal, and special papers are made to withstand the heat of a laser printer and still accept ink. Such paper prints sharper images.

Ask the printer if the resolution can be improved by overexposing or underexposing the negative. This process tends to make the image darker, and more ink will be applied during printing.

Ask for discounts. Printers are unregulated, but they are businesspersons. Many offer significant discounts to keep and maintain clients—but if you do not ask for a discount, they will not offer it.

CHAPTER 10

COLOR SEPARATIONS

In Chapter 8, you learned to create Ventura Publisher style sheets. As you know, many different attributes or characteristics can be assigned to a style sheet. One use of style sheets is to make color separations. Before learning to use a style sheet to make color separations, first consider what a color separation is.

A printer inserts a piece of paper into a printing press, and an impression (type, line art, lines, rules, and/or photographic images) is made on the paper. The paper is then removed from the printing press. Black ink is the most commonly used ink.

Suppose you want a second color—red—in your document. The printer would run the same piece of paper through the press a second time, but first, the press must be filled with red ink.

In most cases, you would not want red ink to be printed on top of black ink; instead, you would want some of the document printed in red and other parts in black. The printer needs two versions of the document: one containing elements to be printed in black and a second containing elements to be printed in red. (The same principal works for four-color printing processes).

If you print one page from a laser printer or typesetting service, when you go to the printer, you must tell the printer to print appropriate text or graphics in a separate color. The printer, in turn, makes a color separation, which creates two separate printing plates. The paper will be run through the printing press twice—once for each color.

You can, of course, use Ventura to make one copy of your document and allow the printer to make color separations. If you use Ventura to create your own color separations, you will soon realize many advantages. First, you will be able to see on your computer screen (if you are using a color monitor and a computer with a 80286 or 80386 chip) what the color will look like on your finished document. You decide what portions of your document should have each color. The cost of having the printer perform the color separation is eliminated, and it should take less time because the printer needs only to print the finished job.

VENTURA PUBLISHER COLORS

Eight colors are available in Ventura: white, black, red, green, blue, cyan, yellow, and magenta. Colors can be assigned to paragraph tags, ruling lines, box around, graphics, frames, and almost any element in Ventura. How colors appear on the screen or printed page depends on what monitor and printer you are using.

Of course, when you take camera-ready copy to a printer, you can specify any available ink color. The printer's ink—not Ventura—determines the final color of the document.

COLOR STYLE SHEETS

A two-color separation requires three Ventura style sheets. A three-color separation requires four style sheets. These style sheets are identical except for colors assigned to each tag.

The first style sheet is the master style sheet in which you can see exactly how everything will look when finished. You can assign colors to different tags to see an approximation on screen of how they will look when printed. After you have determined the color to be assigned to each element, change all tags to black. This is now the master style sheet.

USING
COLOR
SEPARATIONS

Learning how to use color separations is easy with Ventura Publisher. The ability to change the color of the text permits you to quickly and easily make color separations.

In this example, we simply tagged the headline, and selected the color red. We also chose red for the rules that appear on the page. The body text remained in black.

We then followed the steps as outlined in this chapter, then printed the pages. You are reading the results.

Making color separations is easy with Ventura. This figure shows an example of a brochure to be printed in color. The headline and ruling lines will be red (shown in gray here), and the body text will be black. These colors are selected in the Font and Ruling Lines dialog boxes under Ventura's Paragraph menu heading.

Figure 10.1

The next version of the style sheet is the black style sheet. Because most of your documents are primarily black, always start with the black style sheet. Tag all paragraphs and rules that are not to be printed in black. Assign white text to those paragraph tags. Text and rules assigned white are still there, but you will not see them. The next step is to save this style sheet as the black style sheet.

Learning how to use color separations is easy with Ventura Publisher. The ability to change the color of the text permits you to quickly and easily make color separations.

In this example, we simply tagged the headline, and selected the color red. We also chose red for the rules that appear on the page. The body text remained in black.

We then followed the steps as outlined in this chapter, then printed the pages. You are reading the results.

In this example, only black text is printed. The headline and rules have been tagged with white for color. The printer would print only this text with black ink.

Figure 10.2

For the next color, you need yet another version of the style sheet — the red style sheet. Retrieve the master style sheet, and change the color of the text to be printed in red from black to red. Change the remaining text and rules to white. Then, save this style sheet as the red style sheet. This procedure can be repeated for other colors if you want more than two.

USING
COLOR
SEPARATIONS

This page shows the type and rules that have been tagged with red color (black here). The body text has now been tagged white. The printer would print this page in red.

Figure 10.3

When you are finished, print each style sheet. The master style sheet—though in black—will show you the layout of the finished document. The red style sheet will show only text to be printed in red. The black style sheet will display only text to be printed in black. Only the red and black style sheets are given to the printer for reproduction.

At first, it may seem like a lot of work to create color separation style sheets. It takes time, just as creating any style sheet does, but it need only be performed once. Then, each time you are going to produce color separations, you need only import text and graphics into your color style sheets.

CROP MARKS

In Ventura's Printing menu, you have the option to turn on crop marks. In most cases, when working with color separations, you should use crop marks. The printer will use these marks to align the paper each time it is fed through the press. These marks must then be trimmed from the printed paper. For tight alignment (such as two-color trademarks, rules, and text) crop marks must be used to achieve maximum results. For jobs where tight alignment may not be necessary (brochures, bulletins, announcements), crop marks may not be necessary. If you don't use crop marks, the printer is not forced to trim the paper.

NAMING COLOR SEPARATION STYLE SHEETS

If you are using color style sheets, you should include the color in the style sheet's name. Following are possible names and descriptions of color style sheets:

MR-NEWS1.STY	Master Style Sheet—Newsletter #1
BK-NEWS1.STY	Black Style Sheet—Newsletter #1
RE-NEWS1.STY	Red Style Sheet—Newsletter #1
GR-NEWS1.STY	Green Style Sheet—Newsletter #1
BL-NEWS1.STY	Blue Style Sheet—Newsletter #1
CY-NEWS1.STY	Cyan Style Sheet—Newsletter #1
YE-NEWS1.STY	Yellow Style Sheet—Newsletter #1
MA-NEWS1.STY	Magenta Style Sheet—Newsletter #1

FOUR-COLOR SEPARATIONS

Four-color work requires five style sheets: master, cyan, magenta, yellow, and black. These four colors are used by printers to produce a wide range of printed colors. If halftones are used, a color photo can be reproduced with printing methods.

You will not be using Ventura to work on the color separation of the photo; the printer will perform that task with scanners. For pages in which you want black text, a color border, a box around the color picture, and a color dialog box, you can use this process to prepare the non-photo separation. When completed, take the four color separation sheets—cyan, magenta, yellow, and black—along with the color photo to the printer for reproduction.

WHITE TEXT AND LASER PRINTERS

Some laser printers will not accept white text. They simply print it as black text. If your laser printer treats white text as black text, you will not be able to produce color separations using this procedure.

In such cases, all you can do is place frames in the text, delete red text in the black style sheet, and then create a red style sheet by deleting black text.

COLOR FRAMES

In Ventura's Frame menu, the last selection—Frame Background—allows you to assign a color to a frame's background. You can choose one of Ventura's colors, and you can also choose the pattern.

For **text pulls** (important passages extracted from text, which are frequently boxed and set in larger type to draw readers into a document), use of color frames increases design possibilities. If you assign the frame background a color other than black, you can have a color background printed on your sheet for the text pull. For example, if you are using a blue line on the top and bottom of the page, you can assign a blue background to a frame. When you print the blue style sheet (which contains all elements to be printed in blue), the frame will include a blue background.

Use a light pattern—a setting of 1 or 2—to prevent the background of this blue box from being too blue and making the text difficult or impossible to read.

These types of color frames can also be created for side bars or framed boxes to add style and color to your printed pages.

CHAPTER 11

PHOTOGRAPHS

For desktop publishers, importing and printing photographs is a technological challenge. The tiny dots printed by a laser printer — 90,000 per square inch — are only available in one size and color. As mentioned in Chapters 5 and 6, the laser printer must create gray scales using only those black dots. Because of the limitations of the dot size, photos printed on a laser printer are usually grainy and not of the highest quality.

Photographs — both negatives and prints — are **continuous tone images**, which means the tones range from black to white. In regular printing processes, ink cannot be varied in grayness to re-create these tones; instead, the printer prints tiny dots of solid black. These dots are so tiny they look gray when mixed with white space.

Before the printer can reproduce a photograph, it must be converted into many small dots. This process of creating gray tones is called **halftoning**. A halftone works by varying the size of the dots; larger dots print more ink and create darker tones than smaller dots.

The **screen** size determines the size of the dots. Don't confuse this term with your computer's monitor, or screen. In this case, a numbered screen is placed over the photograph. Larger screen numbers indicate smaller dots in higher quantities (e.g., a 200-line screen will produce a finer reproduction than a 100-line screen).

BLACK-AND-WHITE PHOTOGRAPHS

Working with black-and-white photographs provides several options. The traditional method involves creating a frame in which you want the picture to appear in your document. Place a box around the frame. Then, print your document. (See Figure 11.1.) Take the output and the photograph to the printer. The printer makes a screened print (sometimes called a Velox, a stat, a positive halftone, or a PMT). Usually at a cost of $5 to $10, the stat can then be cropped, cut, positioned, and pasted within the frame in your document. The printer can then take a picture of the camera-ready document.

ADVERTISING CAMPAIGN

THE JOLLIE MOLLIE PROMOTION

for

THE TWISTER PRETZELS SNACK

Prepared for the Pennsylvania Food Corporation

AN OVERVIEW:
In April, a new snack food will be introduced and marketed

Photographs add dimension to your document. In the frame, a picture of Jollie Mollie will add impact, attention, and interest to the first page of the example advertising campaign report in Appendix B.

Figure 11.1

There are additional considerations when using black-and-white photographs in Ventura:

1. Sometimes, you can have stats made at a graphics camera business. Look in the phone book under Printing Plates and Typesetting Services. These are the same services many printers in your area use to make stats. You may be able to save money by arranging these services yourself.

2. Use black-and-white film (not color) for photographs.

3. Use high-speed film (such as Kodak Tri-X) for better gray shades, darker blacks, and whiter whites.

4. Avoid harsh shadows caused by flashes. Use natural light; when you must use a flash, use a bounce flash.

5. Select photographs carefully. Just as it takes a talented writer to create good writing, it takes a masterful photographer to make master photographs.

6. Crop photographs effectively. **Cropping** is a design technique that involves cutting out the elements of a photograph that detract from the main element you want to emphasize. For example, you might choose to cut out people in the background of a photograph. Even minimal cropping often improves a photograph dramatically.

7. Choose photographs with plain backgrounds. Backgrounds filled with distracting images distract from images you want to emphasize.

Simple, plain backgrounds call all the attention to the subject.

Figure 11.2

8. Learn about photography. There are hundreds of books available at your library on the subject, which is far beyond the scope of this book.

9. Use proof sheets to save money. This way, you can examine all images and choose the best to be enlarged for reproduction.

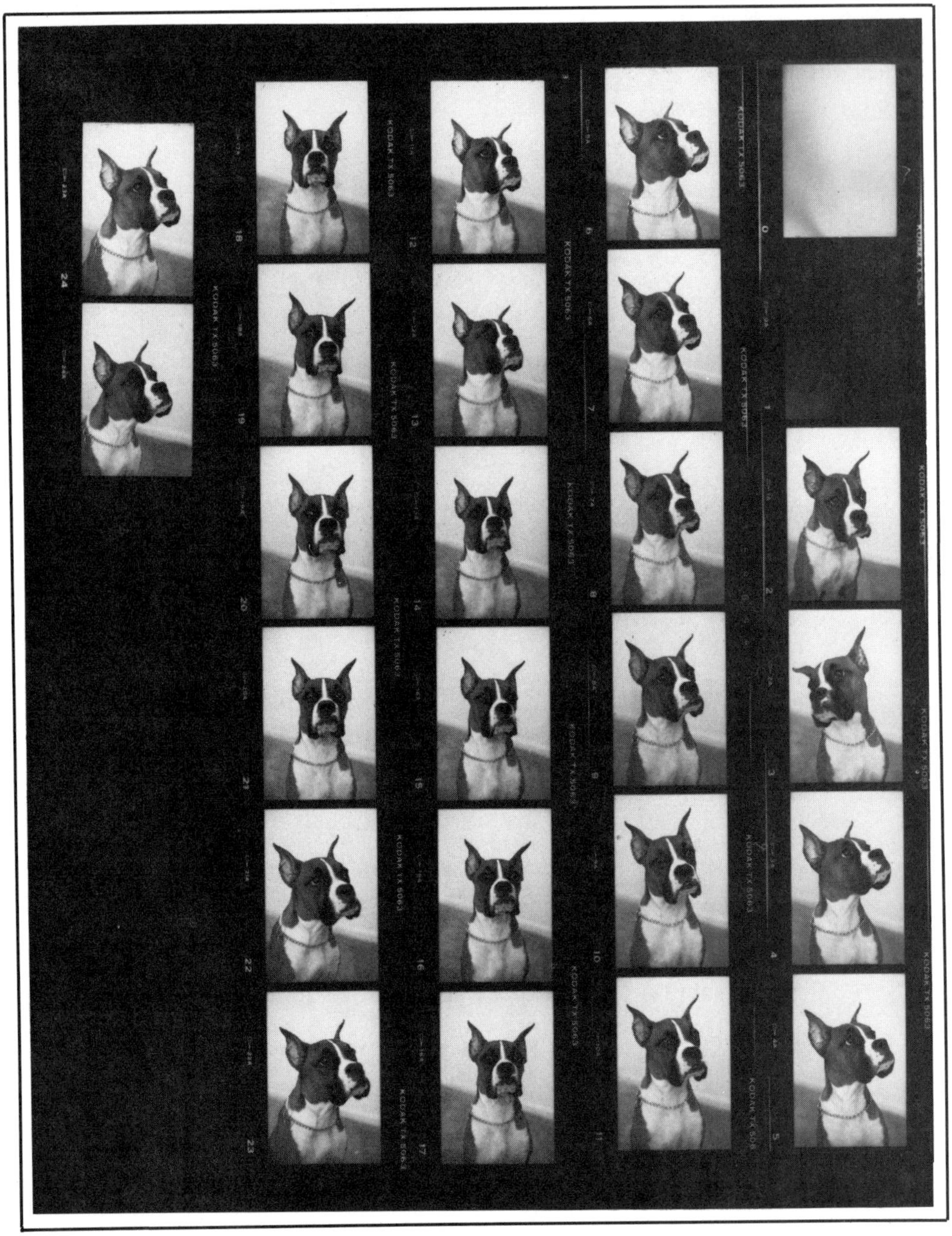

Proof sheets can save you time and money. This figure shows the proof sheet used to select the picture of Jollie Mollie for the example report in Appendix B.

Figure 11.3

10. Never use photographs that are "almost perfect." Photos that could have had "this done differently" or "that changed" are not good enough.

11. Choose the right screen. Screens are slanted 45 degrees so the printed dots are not visible. If the dots were placed on a 90-degree angle, the dots would be more visible. Screens vary from 50 to 300 lines per inch.

12. Choose a screen based on the type of printing press on which your final document will be printed. If you are printing an advertisement on newsprint with a web press, a 65-line screen is adequate. If the photograph is being reproduced on glossy paper stock of magazine quality, consider a 133-line screen. Rough paper (such as newsprint) cannot accomodate a higher-screen photograph because the dots are too close, and the ink runs together.

13. Photos can be "bled" off the side of the paper for effect. This technique is used quite often on magazine covers.

14. Use original photographs and negatives when available. Duplication often creates a fuzzy image.

15. The same process used for printing photographs can be used for non-photographic artwork. Your artist's original work can be made into a stat and pasted into a Ventura frame.

16. If you are going to be pasting photos or artwork to make them camera-ready, use regular paste-up board; it is thicker and easier to use than paper.

17. Seek professional advice on which screens to use for your photographs.

18. If you will be using several photos of basically the same gray scale range, and if they require the same amount of reduction or enlargement, you can paste them on one large sheet and have the entire sheet made into a stat. You can then cut and paste these photographs as needed. This process will save you money.

COLOR PHOTOGRAPHS

There is currently no way to digitize or scan a color photograph into present-generation desktop publishing systems. You can scan a color photograph, but it will print in black and white from the laser printer. If you must create a document that will include color photos, you can use Ventura to create the typesetting and line-art images. Again, make frames where the photographs are to appear in the finished, printed work. Then, take the photographs (preferably color transparencies—color prints only if necessary) to the printer.

DIGITIZED OR SCANNED PHOTOGRAPHS

Desktop publishers can scan photographs and convert them to bit-mapped images. Using a video camera—and a monitor to freeze and position the image—you can use a video signal to create a bit-format image. Two such systems are currently available—Publisher's ImageMaker and Aldus' SnapShot. You can create Encapsulated PostScript (EPS) image files that can then be imported into Ventura.

Of course, you can load pictures into paint-and-draw programs and edit them by turning on and off individual pixels.

Scanning systems are not for everyone. The cost—several thousand dollars for a camera, lens, monitor, cable, software, and controller board—makes these systems beyond the reach of many desktop publishers. Even after you capture the image, the lack of various-size dots from a laser printer makes images look as if they were printed with a 50- or 60-line screen. The results will not be as good as taking a photograph and having a stat created.

However, there are many applications in which a scanned photo will be adequate. For instructional manuals, workbooks, brochures, internal documents, product development, and government work, these systems can do the job. Once again, when speed is a factor, consider the control placed in your hands by such systems. For sensitive, confidential information, photographs can be taken, printed, and controlled without leaving your office or production facilities. Again, the output will not be as precise as a typical photograph published in a magazine, but the cost will be less.

Make sure that scanned image files are in .IMG format. They can be imported into Ventura chapters much like any other document, text, line art, or image.

PHOTOGRAPHS AND DESKTOP PUBLISHING

The decision to use a stat will depend on the intended quality, control, time, and budget for a job. Just because you are limited with photographs in desktop publishing doesn't mean you should not use them. Page through a book. When you see a photograph or drawing, you naturally stop at that page and look at it. Do not overlook the power of photography to sell, motivate, or capture your reader's interest. Photographs attract attention, explain, and set a document's mood.

Use Ventura to position those photos on your pages. One trick to help visualize images on your pages is to temporarily change the frame background to a darker shade. By doing so, you will see darkened squares on your page in the Reduced View mode.

CHAPTER 12

WORKING FASTER WITH VENTURA

Learning to work faster with Ventura will save time and help you become a better desktop publisher. There are simple techniques for working faster with Ventura. You can rush out and purchase a Compaq Deskpro 386/20—the speed demon of computers. Even a machine such as this will not eliminate the need to work faster with Ventura. Working faster actually means working smarter, which is always a worthy goal.

SPECIAL TIPS FOR INCREASED PERFORMANCE

Following are tips to help you work faster with Ventura:

1. Plan your work carefully. The old-fashioned pencil and paper can be worth their weight in gold. Avoid unnecessary delays by knowing what you want to create before you start.

2. Create all files to be imported *before* you start Ventura. Make sure all text and graphic files have been generated and are ready for use in Ventura. This eliminates unnecessary delays caused by leaving Ventura to create another graphic or text file.

3. Use the Speed Disk utility included with the Norton Utilities Advanced Version 4.0 software package. This program will reorganize your hard disk to increase performance.

4. Learn to use all keyboard shortcuts. They save time and eliminate the need to drag the mouse to a menu and then drag through the menu to a dialog box. To use the following Ventura keyboard shortcuts, press the key or simultaneously press the key combinations indicated below:

Add Frame, Tag, or Set Font	Ctrl/2
Assign Function Keys	Ctrl/K
Bring to Front (graphics)	Ctrl/A
Copy	Shift/Del
Copyright (©)	Ctrl/Shift/C
Cut	Del
Delete—left of the text cursor	Backspace
Delete—right of the text cursor	Del

continued...

...from previous page

Delete Selection line text	Esc
Discretionary hyphen	Ctrl/hyphen
Double quote, closing	Ctrl/Shift/]
Double quote, opening	Ctrl/Shift/[
EM dash	Ctrl/]
EM space	Ctrl/Shift/M
EN dash	Ctrl/[
EN space	Ctrl/Shift/N
Enlarged View	Ctrl/E
Figure space	Ctrl/Shift/F
Fill Attributes	Ctrl/F
Frame Setting Function	Ctrl/U
Go to Page	Ctrl/G
Go to first page	Home
Go to last page	End
Go to next page	PgDn
Go to previous page	PgUp
Graphic Drawing Function	Ctrl/P
Line Attributes	Ctrl/L
Line Break	Ctrl/Enter
Non-breaking Space	Ctrl/Spacebar
Normal View	Ctrl/N
Paragraph Tagging Function	Ctrl/|
Paste	Ins
Recall last dialog box	Ctrl/X
Reduced View	Ctr/R
Registered trademark	Ctrl/Shift/R
Renumber Chapter	Ctrl/B
Savc	Ctrl/S
Select All (graphics)	Ctrl/Q
Send to Back	Ctrl/Z
Show/Hide Tabs & Returns	Ctrl/T
Show/Hide Side-Bar	Ctrl/W
Text Editing Function	Ctrl/O
Thin space	Ctrl/Shift/T
Trademark	Ctrl/Shift/2

Of particular interest is the Ctrl/X key combination, which accesses the last dialog box in which you were working. This command can save you much time when experimenting with page layout. By using this command, you can make attribute changes quickly and compare how different characteristics will eventually appear. Again, this technique eliminates moving the mouse cursor and pulling down a menu to access a dialog box.

5. Adjust mouse speed to your own preference. In most cases, as you become more experienced with using a mouse in Ventura, you will find that you can easily increase the double-click speed (under Preferences in the Options menu). If you increase the double-click speed, Ventura will also respond faster when you press Enter.

6. Use a double-click to select items in a selection box. This technique also will eliminate the need to press Return or move the mouse cursor to OK and click the button.

7. Do not use other RAM-resident programs with Ventura. Although many will work with Ventura, they will only slow its operation.

8. Use a small block of text—no more than one page—to build the style sheet. Text is needed only to review the assigned attributes.

9. Build your style sheets first. Then, import all text and art.

10. Use **greeked** text to increase screen drawing speed when text is too small to be legible. Greeked text is generic or "fake" text used for display purposes only. It allows you to concentrate on the overall appearance of your text without having to wait as long for the screen to refresh when you make changes. The numbers in the Text to Greek setting in the Set Preferences dialog box under the Options menu are for pixels—not point sizes. Use the largest number for maximum greeking.

11. Turning off on-screen graphics will result in remarkable speed improvements. Select Hide Pictures in the Options menu.

12. Use function keys to quickly tag paragraphs. Press Ctrl-K to assign paragraph tags to the function keys.

13. Use the Shift key to tag more than one paragraph. Although you can only select paragraphs on one page at a time, by using the Shift key, you can highlight more than one paragraph at a time. Then, use the appropriate function key to assign the paragraph tag.

14. Learn to use both hands. For right-handed persons: keep your right hand on the mouse and your left hand on the keyboard. For left-handed persons: keep the mouse in your left hand and keep your right hand on the keyboard. Use your keyboard hand to press function keys.

15. Press Return instead of using the mouse to click on OK. In any Ventura dialog box in which you see OK, you can press Return to select your options.

16. Turn off on-screen kerning in the Set Preferences dialog box of the Options menu. This function is only needed for special work with large typefaces. For general work, turn off on-screen kerning.

17. Import all files needed in one operation. In the Load Text/Picture dialog box, select Several for # of files. Then, select all files to be imported.

18. Use the PgDn, PgUp, Home, and End keys to change pages and move rapidly through a Ventura chapter.

19. Learn to use Ventura's Multi-chapter function in the Options menu, which allows you to combine a large number of chapters into a single publication.

20. Press Ctrl-K to remind you of the paragraph tag names assigned to each function key.

21. Do not alter original Ventura style sheets. They should be preserved so you can quickly build chapters from standard examples.

22. Insert the paragraph filter in the beginning of each text file. As discussed in Chapter 3, the parafilter command eliminates the need to remove extra carriage returns in text. The parafilter command is @PARAFILTER ON =.

23. Develop and reuse layouts. After you develop a layout and use it often, it will become easier to work with.

24. Use the Shift-select technique when working with the mouse in your text. You may occasionally find it difficult to highlight exactly the text you want with the mouse alone. Move the mouse so the cursor is at the position where you want the additional text selected. Then, press and hold down the Shift key, and click the mouse while moving it in the direction you want. The selected text area can be expanded one character at a time.

25. Work in picas and points rather than inches. Although you are probably more familiar with inches than picas, picas seldom must be divided in half or expressed in fractional measures.

26. Prepare files with proper extensions for importing. For example, if you are importing WordPerfect text files, add .WP as the file extension. If you are importing a Lotus 1-2-3 spreadsheet, make sure you first convert the spreadsheet to ASCII text by printing the file to the disk and creating a spreadsheet file with the extension .PRN. Don't forget to change the extension to .TXT to import ASCII text into Ventura.

27. Load a chapter as you start Ventura Publisher. For example, if you want to start with the chapter named BOOK4 on the C drive in the C:\BOOKS subdirectory, type the following command at the DOS prompt:

    VP C:\BOOKS\BOOK4.CHP

28. Use the parallel printer port rather than the serial port, if available. Ventura works faster if you use the parallel port.

29. Working with tabs can be tricky. If you are importing a Lotus 1-2-3 spreadsheet, use one of the conversion programs mentioned in Chapter 16 to convert the spreadsheet into an easily aligned format. Use Ventura tab settings—not word processor tabs—to align text. Remember, only one tab should be inserted between items. In your word processor, you may be tempted to add additional tabs to align text. This technique works fine in word processing, but it will not work in Ventura (see Figures 12.1 and 12.2). For example, the following table is correct for importing into Ventura:

Fred Jones[tab]$136.88
Connie Smithe-Garcia[tab]$343.98
G. Lu[tab]$218.33
Samuel J. Schwartzenecker[tab]$359.75
Gloria Laukhuff[tab]$432.12

Notice that one tab (and only one tab) has been inserted after the name and before the amount. You may be tempted to enter the text as follows:

Fred Jones[tab] [tab] [tab] [tab]$136.88
Connie Smithe-Garcia[tab] [tab]$343.98
G. Lu[tab] [tab] [tab] [tab] [tab]$218.33
Samuel J. Schwartzenecker[tab]$359.75
Gloria Laukhuff[tab] [tab] [tab]$432.12

If you do, your text will not align in Ventura.

HOW TO CREATE TEXT TABLES

Step#1 Create the text as shown. Do not use traditional word processing tabs and indents. Rather, the text for a table should be created in regular paragraph format.

Step #2 Import the text in the normal manner.

Step #3 Select the Paragraph tagging icon. Create a new paragraph tag called "ParaLeft." Select Breaks, and choose Before in the Line Break selection.

Step #4 Tag the second paragraph. Add another tag, calling it ParaRight. Select Spacing in the Paragraph menu. Change the indent to In from Left.

Step #5 Select Breaks, and change the Line Break to After

Step #6 Complete the tagging of your paragraphs. When completed, your text should resemble this example.

How text would look if produced in the normal manner in a word processor, using tabs and indents.

Figure 12.1

```
HOW TO CREATE TEXT TABLES

Step#1
Create the text as shown.  Do not use traditional word
processing tabs and indents.  Rather, the text for a table
should be created in regular paragraph format.
Step #2
Import the text in the normal manner.
Step #3
Select the Paragraph tagging icon.  Create a new paragraph tag
called "ParaLeft."  Select Breaks, and choose Before in the Line
Break selection.
Step #4
Tag the second paragraph.  Add another tag, calling it
ParaRight.  Select Spacing in the Paragraph menu. Change the
indent to In from Left.
Step #5
Select Breaks, and change the Line Break to After
Step #6
Complete the tagging of your paragraphs.  When completed, your
text should resemble this example.
```

How the text should look when produced in a word processor for importing into Ventura. No tabs or indents were used.

Figure 12.2

30. When creating tables, it is best to use a separate tag for each column within the table. By creating a separate tag, you can align text in the table by setting appropriate margins. Remember, if you do not want the table to break across the page, use the Breaks Dialog box to prevent the table from crossing the page.

31. Use a line break in tables to separate rows. A line break is inserted by pressing Ctrl-Enter or when creating text by pressing Enter. Remember, when Ventura encounters a line break, it will start a new line—not a new paragraph.

32. Memory problems may occur any time you are working with Ventura. Memory problems will slow Ventura operation. If you are using a computer with less than 640K RAM, consider adding RAM if possible. You can always check available memory by accessing Ventura's Diagnostics box (in the Desk menu, select Publisher Info, and click on the word "Ventura." The Ventura Diagnostics box will appear.) Ventura controls the amount of memory allocated to different functions within the program.

    You can work faster by avoiding memory problems if you keep the following points in mind:

    - Use the Body Text tag for the most-used text in your document.
    - Remove RAM-resident programs (such as SideKick, SuperKey, or HotShot) before starting Ventura.
    - Ventura limits the number of lines on a page. Avoid this problem by not using multiple-column formats with small (e.g., 6-point) type.
    - Save memory by eliminating unused paragraph tags.
    - Avoid long chapters; instead, use the Multi-Chapter feature available in the Options Menu to combine and print smaller chapters.

CHAPTER 13

SPECIAL EFFECTS AND APPLICATIONS

With a little imagination and the right dialog box settings, you can create many special effects in Ventura. This chapter provides instructions on how to create special affects and applications.

LEADER DOTS

Leader dots are often warranted in product listings, directories, price lists, specification sheets, and other such documents. Leader dots guide your reader's eyes across the page from one entry to another. Following is an example:

12 oz. bag..24 per case
18 oz. bag..12 per case
30 oz. bag..10 per case

To create leader dots, use the Tab Settings dialog box, and select ... as the leader character. Remember, there should only be one tab between each data item. Ventura automatically fills the distance with leader dots, based on the tab settings.

THUMB TABS

Thumb tabs are used in books, directories, and reports. They are printed on the very edge of the page and often bleed off the side. Thumb tabs make it easier to use and refer to separate sections of the document.

It is easy to create thumb tabs in Ventura by using the Repeating Frame command under the Frame menu to make the thumb tab appear on each page of your chapter.

If you are using a 1" margin, make the thumb tab .5" wide (horizontally). Thumb tabs can be any length, but they are generally not longer than 2" (vertically).

You can create thumb tabs using the following steps:

1. Enable the Frame mode, and select Add New Frame.
2. Create a small frame on the outer edge of the page.
3. Fill the frame with a dark pattern.
4. Select Repeating Frame.

Thumb tabs show up best when printed on both sides of the page. Move the repeating frame down for each new chapter or section of your publication.

If your laser printer will print white text, you can add text in the repeating frame. For example, the section of your directory containing the "S" and "T" listings could have "S-T" included in the thumb tab.

Thumb tabs work best when they are flush to the edge of the paper. Your laser printer may not be able to print to the very edge of the page. Consider having the finished document trimmed so the thumb tab bleeds off the side of the page or have the printer enlarge the page so the tabs bleed off the side.

WHITE TEXT ON A BLACK RULE (REVERSE TYPE)

Reverse type is white characters printed on a black background. In each of the Ruling Lines menus under the Paragraph menu heading, the Space Below Rule 3 option allows you to shift the entire set of ruling lines up or down by the amount of space that you specify—without moving the text in the tagged paragraph. By using proper settings, you can create a black bar containing white text.

The steps for creating white text on a black rule are as follows:

1. Create a new tag (e.g., WT for white text)

2. Tag the text paragraph to be positioned on the black rule as outlined previously.

3. Change the color of the font to white.

4. Select Ruling Lines Above, and choose a height for Rule 1 that is larger than the text's font size. For example, if you chose 12-point type for the text, you could make the ruling line 18 points wide.

5. In the Ruling Line Above dialog box, select the - (minus) block to the right of the the + (plus) block by moving the mouse cursor to the Space Below Rule 3 option. Then, enter the distance required to move the ruling line down and over the text. To compute the required distance, add the ruling line height plus the font size and divide the result in half. For example, a ruling line height of 18 + a font size of 12 = 30. Thirty divided by 2 = 15 points. Enter 15 in the Space Below Rule 3 block.

SHADED TYPE

Creating shaded type is similar to creating reverse type. Shaded type uses a screen or pattern as a background.

Follow the steps used to create white text on a black rule, but keep the text white, and change the rule pattern (try pattern #2 first).

STYLE LINES AND BLOCKS

Many magazine and newsletter layouts include style lines across the top of the page. To create style lines and blocks, select the underlying page frame. Choose the Ruling Line Above option, and create your lines. Use a repeating frame to maintain this effect on other pages.

LARGER BULLETS

If you want a larger bullet than those provided by Ventura, tag a paragraph and select the Special Effects option from the Paragraph menu. Once you have accessed the Special Effects dialog box, select the Bullet and Set Font Properties options. By choosing a large point size, you create a larger bullet, but the size of text remains unchanged.

LARGE FIRST LETTERS

To create a paragraph with a large first letter, choose the Special Effects option in the Paragraph menu. You can change the size of the paragraph's first letter by selecting a different typeface. You can also adjust the amount of space used by the first letter by changing the indent settings.

FLOWING TEXT AROUND ART

To flow text around art, select the frame and then select the Flow Text Around: Off option. Then, position a series of smaller frames on top of the object, covering the area where you do not want text. Select the Flow Text Around: On option.

TEXT ON AN ANGLE

To position text on an angle, draw a line to position the angle. Then, insert a series of small frames to position the text in the place you want it to appear.

LOGOS OR LINE ART ON EACH PAGE

Position a frame on your page. Then, import logo or line art as usual. Then, select the Repeating Frame option, and choose both left and right pages. The logo or line art will be correctly positioned on each page throughout the document.

MULTIPLE-ARTICLE CHAPTERS

In publications such as newsletters, magazines, and newspapers, it is common to have several articles or stories on one page. Quite often, you will want to start an article on one page and flow the text to another page in the publication. Although this may seem complex, Ventura can easily perform this task.

The first step is to select the number of columns and to establish those columns on your underlying page frame. It is best to use the Snap To Columns function, and it is also easier if you select the Show Column Guides option.

Use the Frame Setting function to insert and position frames on the page where you want the articles to appear. After these frames have been positioned on the page, select the frame and the file name containing the text. The frame can be made larger or smaller to increase or decrease the amount of text displayed.

Unless you are working with very small text files, there will probably be more text to be inserted elsewhere in your publication. To continue the flow of text to another frame from the previous frame, select the new frame, and then select the text file name in the sidebar. The text will continue from the first selected frame to the next—or currently selected—frame.

The second frame can also be placed on the same page as the first frame. You can repeat this method, placing and using as many frames as required by your text.

If you use this method, you will not be placing text on the underlying page frame. Accordingly, Ventura will not create new pages automatically. You must use the Insert New Page option in the Page menu to add new blank pages.

Realize that Ventura places the text in the frame that was first placed on the page and then flows the text into the next pasted frame. You can cut and paste a frame; this procedure makes the frame become the "last" frame. You can change the first frame to the last frame by simply selecting the first frame and then cutting and pasting it. By doing so, you will change the frame containing the first section of your text.

Although you can paste the first section of your text on page 4 and the second section on page 7, you cannot flow from frame to frame in reverse order. In other words, you cannot place the first section on page 7 and the second section on page 4.

PATTERNED BORDERS

You needn't use solid lines to create frame borders. By selecting a pattern, you can create a unique border for pulled text.

When you choose a pattern for your border in the Ruling Box Around dialog box, all rules will be in the chosen pattern. To place a solid rule around the pattern box, create two frames. The larger frame will contain the solid rule. The second, slightly smaller frame, will contain the selected pattern.

UNUSUAL BORDERS

Clip art programs occasionally include unusual borders. You can import the clip art border into a frame and create a second frame in which to import your text.

The Jollie Mollie Promotion consists of using a Boxer dog, named Jollie Mollie, as our advertising mascot. Jollie Mollie, the Boxer Dog, would rather eat a Twister Pretzel Snack, than her dog food. And she would do anything for a Twister Pretzel Snack, including the twister, a special dog dance where she twists and jumps with joy in the anticipation of eating a Twister Pretzel Snack.

An example of a clip art border with imported text.

Figure 13.1

CHAPTER 14

COPYRIGHTS

As a desktop publisher, you can copyright your work. This chapter should provide you with a working knowledge of current copyright laws.

Copyright laws allow desktop publishers to maintain total control over their creative work. A copyright is the exclusive right—granted by the copyright law established by the United States Congress—to prevent anyone else from making an unauthorized copy of your material. Anything you create—books, magazines, newsletters, advertisements, brochures—can be copyrighted.

Copyrighting is complex because it protects "intellectual property." Copyright laws protect creative thoughts and expressions and prevent others from using them without permission. Often, permission is gained when the creator assigns rights to a publisher, and the publisher pays a fee (usually a royalty). Anything you create is exclusively yours and generally cannot be used, published, or reproduced without your permission.

The difference between copyrights and trademarks is that a copyright protects original ideas, while a trademark protects a word, slogan, name, or symbol used by a company to identify its products. For example, IBM is the registered trademark of the International Business Machines Corp. A registered trademark is claimed by adding the ® symbol to the trademark (e.g., IBM®).

Congress passed the original United States Copyright law in 1909. In 1976, the United States Congress passed a new copyright law that became effective January 1, 1978. (A brief history of the law and its highlights can be found in Copyright Office Circular R99.)

COPYRIGHT LAW BASICS

The basic elements of copyright law are as follows:

Everything you create is exclusively yours. You are the copyright owner from the moment of creation. Copyright protects an expression of an idea—not the idea itself. You cannot, for example, copyright an idea about a tough street fighter who gets a once-in-a-lifetime chance to be a prizefighter. You can, however, copyright the actual story, which is exactly what Sylvester Stallone did with the script for the movie *Rocky*.

You must place a notice on your documents that the material is copyrighted. The copyright notice must contain the word Copyright, the abbreviation Copr., or the copyright symbol ©. The notice must also include the year the work was published or, if it is unpublished, the year it was finished, and name of the person or company claiming the copyright. This notice must be affixed in such a manner "as to give reasonable notice of the claim of copyright."

This notice must appear in one of the following three forms:

Copyright 1988 by George Sheldon
Copr. 1988 by George Sheldon
© 1988 by George Sheldon

Placing a C in parentheses is not a valid copyright notice. The following notice would not be considered valid by a court:

(C) 1988 by George Sheldon

For protection in countries that have not signed the International Copyright Convention Agreement (including many Latin American countries), you can protect your work by adding the phrase "All Rights Reserved."

Copyright owners are not required to register their work with the Library of Congress Copyright Office to receive copyright protection; however, it is recommended that you do so. If you register work, you can prove your copyright in court. A registered copyright not only serves as proof before a court of law, but it is almost always required before the FBI will investigate a criminal violation of copyright law. (Both criminal and civil penalties are attached to copyright law.)

Copyright protection generally lasts fifty years beyond the life of the creator.

In most cases, desktop publishers should use Form TX or Form SE to register a copyright with the Copyright Office. These forms include detailed instructions and, when compared with other government forms, are fairly simple to complete. When registering your work, there is a $10 fee, and you must also furnish two copies of the published work or one photocopy of an unpublished work.

You can register a collection of work—a series of pamphlets, newsletters, magazines, etc.—at the same time and on the same form, all for the $10 fee, which can save time and money.

In the form, you will given the option of permitting the Library of Congress to reproduce your materials for use by blind or physically handicapped individuals.

Note: A large body of law deals with the Work For Hire doctrine. If you are working for someone else, before you begin, you and your employer should decide in writing who will retain the copyright of your work.

AVOIDING COPYRIGHT PROBLEMS

As a desktop publisher, you must be certain not to infringe upon the copyright of others; if you do, you can be sued and/or criminally prosecuted.

You can freely publish whatever you create, however, or you can publish whatever you obtain permission from the copyright owner to use. As a publisher, you can occasionally obtain permission without paying royalties; other times, you must pay a fee or royalty. For example, the copyright holder of this book could grant you the right to publish only one chapter or to publish this work in another language.

Anyone can freely publish material in the public domain (work for which the copyright has elapsed). An example is the Bible. You can publish the Bible in part or in its entirety without infringing upon a copyright. Always be certain a work is in the public domain before using it without permission.

You can publish a portion of a protected work under the Fair Use doctrine granted in the Copyright law. The Fair Use doctrine permits the use of portions of a protected work, but the definition of "fair use" is determined by the court.

If you publish a copyrighted photograph, it is not fair use because you published the entire work. If you publish three sentences from a 1000-page book, it would probably not be considered a copyright infringement; however, if those few sentences are the very essence of the book, you may find yourself sitting on the losing side of a court case.

Be careful. It is always best to obtain permission to use even a small part of someone else's work. Often, permission can be obtained without paying a royalty. If you will just use a few sentences, many copyright holders will recognize an opportunity for free publicity and grant permission—as long as you agree to publish the source. You can investigate the copyright status of a work by following the instructions in Circular R22.

WORKING WITH THE COPYRIGHT OFFICE

The personnel at the copyright office are quite helpful, and they can answer your non-legal questions about the copyright law. Obviously, if a legal issue arises, seek an attorney experienced in copyright law.

You can write to the Copyright Office at the following address:

Register of Copyrights
Copyright Office
Library of Congress
Washington, D.C. 20559

You can also call the copyright office during normal business hours. The Copyright Public Information Office is (202) 287-7000.

You can order forms from the Copyright Office by calling (202) 287-9100. You can leave a recorded message, and your forms will arrive later by mail, usually within two to three weeks. You can order your forms 24 hours a day, seven days a week.

When calling to order forms for the first time, you ask for Circular 1 and Circular 2. Information contained in these circulars is valuable to all desktop publishers.

The Copyright Office receives and processes over 500,000 copyright registration applications each year. It can take up to 16 weeks to receive notice that your copyright registration was accepted and deposited in the Copyright Office, but your registration is effective from the date the Copyright Office receives your completed application, fee, and deposit (the one or two copies of your work).

You must deposit actual complete samples of your published work (although non-published work can also be copyrighted). You cannot submit photocopies or galleys of published work.

Because of recent budget cuts, the Copyright Office also accepts clean, quality photocopies of its forms. If you plan to register many different works, it may be faster to make copies of the original form. Many of these forms are also available in your local library.

Use the following forms for initial registration:

- Form TX—for published and unpublished nondramatic literary works.
- Form SE—for serials, such as periodicals, newspapers, magazines, newsletters, annuals, journals.

The following circulars are of particular interest to desktop publishers:

Circular	**Topic**
1	Copyright Basics
2	Publications on Copyright
3	Copyright Notice
4	Copyright Fees
62	Copy Registration for Serials on Form SE

The forms are free of charge, but they are available in limited quantities. Many more forms, circulars, and brochures are available, such as information kits dealing with specific areas of copyright. All forms available from the Copyright Office are fully described in Circular 2.

CHAPTER 15

USING SERVICE BUREAUS

You probably realize the value of high-resolution output. At 300 dpi—the current standard for laser printers—the resolution may be too low for some jobs. Unless you plan to install a commercial typesetting machine, you must do one of two things—use the laser printer output or send files to a service bureau for production.

For many jobs, a laser printer can produce sufficient output. You must determine how high the final output's resolution must be. For internal memos, newsletters, product sheets, catalog listings, directories, and even books, laser printer output—even at 300 dpi—may be quite adequate.

For jobs in which prestige is important, such as magazines, corporate reports, consumer or customer product sheets, and sales brochures, high-resolution output—1270 or 2540 dpi—is required. For such jobs, you must contact a service bureau.

Desktop publishers use service bureaus because few are willing to invest $30,000 to $50,000 for commercial typesetting equipment.

Service bureaus are no longer simply companies that own a Linotronic typesetting machine and are looking for type to set. Service bureaus are rapidly expanding, becoming more competitive, and offering additional services. Some service bureaus rent laser printer time. Others design and develop Ventura style sheets, and still others can arrange for printing.

Some service bureaus specialize in Macintosh applications; others specialize in Ventura and DOS applications. Make sure the service bureau you choose has Ventura experience.

BASIC GUIDELINES

Following are guidelines for working with service bureaus:

1. A service bureau must provide service. If you find that a service bureau is too busy to help answer questions or offer suggestions, find another service bureau.

2. Price should not be your primary concern when comparing service bureaus. A low price for poor service is not a bargain. Service comes first, and you may have to pay a little more for better service.

3. Services bureau prices have been decreasing—primarily due to stiffer competition.

4. Many service bureaus have a minimum charge. Group small jobs whenever possible.

5. If you will have a large volume of work for a service bureau, ask for and be ready to negotiate for a lower price. Most service bureaus will bid for high-volume work.

6. Many service bureaus charge more for graphics- and image-filled pages because it takes more time to print these types of pages than regular text pages.

7. Service bureaus can supply output on film or paper. Ask your printer if the price will decrease if you deliver film output.

8. Experiment with service bureaus. Do not experiment with large, important jobs. Give a service bureau small jobs at first to test their service.

9. Do not forget to send complete sets of Ventura files to service bureaus. Remember, Ventura uses a series of files to create chapters. Send all related files.

10. For the first several submissions to a service bureau, send files on diskettes—not by modem. Once you have successfully received decent service through diskette submission, experiment with modem file submission.

11. When you are ready to use a modem to send your files, consider using good communications software, such as Microstuf's Crosstalk Mk.4, which offers automatic scripts and a learning feature to help you quickly access a service bureau's computer.

12. Call a service bureau during non-peak periods to save long-distance modem charges. A service bureau should offer off-hour submission or a 1-800 toll-free number.

13. If your telephone is equipped with call waiting, you should disable this feature before transmitting files via modems. For push-button phones, you can dial *70 to disable call waiting; the feature reactivates as soon as you hang up the receiver. If you are using a rotary phone, dial 1170 to disable call waiting.

14. Use a 1200- or 2400-baud transmission rate (if available) to submit files via modem. The faster the baud rate, the cheaper your long-distance phone bill.

15. Choose a service bureau for service—not geographic location. With many companies clamoring for your overnight-delivery business, a service bureau across the country is only an overnight delivery away.

16. Of course, if you have time, first-class mail will save you money compared to overnight shipping.

17. Service bureaus can provide extra services, such as sending your output directly to the printing company of your choice. Some service bureaus also perform design, layout, and production consulting.

18. Some service bureaus recommend printers. Other service bureaus also provide discount printing services to desktop publishers.

19. Compare pricing. If it costs more for 2540-dpi resolution (and it usually will), determine if such high resolution is necessary. In many cases, you will only need 1270 dpi. A reputable service bureau should be able to help you decide.

20. Always keep in mind a reliable backup service bureau for emergencies. Breakdowns do occur, and when you are in a hurry, it helps to have more than one service available to handle your work.

21. Hairlines, outline typefaces, and 10% screens do not print very well at higher resolutions. Use at least 20% screens, and avoid outline typefaces. Use heavier rules—not hairline widths.

22. If you are using Hewlett-Packard LaserJet output to proof your documents before you send chapters to a service bureau, remember to convert the documents for a PostScript printer in Ventura by selecting PostScript as the Device Name in the Set Printer Info. dialog box under the Options menu heading. You must also make the correct Output To selection, and set the Width Table option to PostScript in the Set Printer Info. dialog box. You must use the PostScript driver to run a Linotronic.

23. Although a laser printer cannot print to the edge of paper, a Linotronic can because it uses 12"-wide paper, which means you can produce 11" × 17" camera-ready documents.

24. Do not use spaces to align type. Even though the proper alignment might occur on the screen, when printed, proportional text will not align unless tabs are used.

25. Always make a copy of your diskette(s) before sending them to a service bureau. Make sure to write ELECTRONIC MEDIA ENCLOSED—DO NOT X-RAY! in bright red on the mailing envelope.

26. Before sending a 3.5" or a 1.2MB high-density 5.25" diskette, make sure the service bureau can accomodate those disk sizes.

27. Numerous typefaces are usually available from a service bureau, and most service bureaus will supply sample output of the different typefaces they offer.

28. Some service bureaus will provide—free of charge—screen fonts of the various PostScript typefaces they have—if you provide the diskettes.

29. Always proofread a hard copy of your work carefully before sending it to a service bureau. Many times, what looks great on the screen looks bad when printed. If you send error-filled files to a service bureau, you will be paying for wasted typesetting services.

30. Make sure fonts in your document match fonts in the typesetting equipment. Hundreds of typefaces are available, and many have similar names. Although they may appear comparable, they can differ enough to create havoc with line endings and paragraphs.

31. Line screens appear darker from a laser printer than they do from a typesetter. Do not use the laser printer as a judgement for your screens. Instead, use samples provided by the service bureau.

32. PostScript-driven devices are often slow. Some service bureaus charge by the hour, and you may be paying more to include bit-mapped graphics. It may be faster—and cheaper—to strip in (paste) your visuals.

33. Some service bureaus offer scanning services. If you do not have a scanner and need an image scanned, make sure that you can import it into your document, which will allow you to crop and size the scanned image if needed.

34. Keep in touch with your service bureau on a regular basis. Many constantly add new services and can answer quesitons and offer suggestions.

PRINTING TO A DISK

In the Options menu, under the Set Printer Info selection, you can print a file to a disk. Simply choose Filename from the Output To selection before printing. If you want Ventura to perform a multiple-chapter print, select the Multi-chapter option from the Options menu; otherwise, simply choose the To Print option under the File menu heading. Ventura will prompt you for the name of the file in which you want the chapter to be printed and saved. If you are printing more than one chapter, you can specify if you want each individual chapter in its own file, or you can print them as multiple Ventura chapters to one large file. You can then send this file to the service bureau for printing.

RESOURCE LIST

Following is a selective list of service bureaus in alphabetical order:

Advanti
415 N. Washington Avenue
Scranton, PA 18503
(717) 761-6183

Alphagraphics
845 E. Broady
Tucson, AZ 85719
(602) 293-9200

Ampersand Typographers
176 Wicksteed Avenue
Toronto, Ontario M4G 2B6
(416) 422-1444

Design Access,Inc.
1770 Union Street
San Francisco, CA 94109
(415) 885-3156

Graphics Plus
Suite 216
3710 South Robertson Blvd.
Culver City, CA 90232
(213) 559-3732

Krishna Copy Center
211 University Avenue
Berkeley, CA 94704
(415) 540-5959

Laser Printing Services
26058 W. 12-Mile Road
Southfield, MI 48034
(313) 477-2733

MacTypeNet
P.O. Box 52188
Livonia, MI 48152-0188
(313) 477-2733

microPRINT
66 Kearny Street
San Francisco, CA 94108
(415) 986-6161

P/S Desktop Publishing Center
17300 E. 17th St., Ste. C
Tustin, CA 92680
(714) 544-1345

Publishing Resources, Inc.
1795 Pearl Street
Boulder, CO 80302
(303) 442-1100

continued...

...from previous page

Rapid Transmit
8007 Douglas Avenue
Racine, WI 53402
(414) 639-2080

Typegraphics
605 Chase Drive, Suite 1B
Tyler, TX 75701
(214) 561-0093

Typeline
668 Front Street
Teaneck, NJ 07666
(201) 836-2300

Typesetting Service Corp.
50 Clifford Street
Providence, RI 02903
(401) 421-2264

Typography Express, Inc.
1230 Grant Avenue, #229
San Francisco, CA 94133
(415) 362-8223

CHAPTER 16

VENTURA PUBLISHER ADD-ONS

Several utility programs can be added to Ventura Publisher to make your work easier. (Complete product information is listed in Chapter 17.)

VP/SADDLE

From The Laser Edge, VP/Saddle offers three special formats:

Two-Up This format prints two side-by-side copies of the same half-size page, on a single sheet of paper. (See Chapter 9 for more information). This format can save thousands of dollars in printing costs.

Saddle-Stitch Named for the stapling technique often used to bind booklets, this format prints two different half-size pages side by side on one sheet of paper. The program pairs pages so they will print in the proper order for being folded to make the booklet. Without this program, Ventura will not output such pages in the correct order for saddle stitching. This program is a must if you are publishing booklets with half-size pages on a PostScript printer.

Enlarged This format enlarges a half-size page image to fill an entire 8.5" × 11" sheet of paper. This program can be used when the final pages are to be offset printed instead of photocopied and will often improve the quality of the printing. This program works for documents that will have a final size of less than 8.5" × 11". For example VP/Saddle enlarges a paperback book (which is 6" × 9") by 122%. The PostScript printer then reduces the page to 82%. In this way, characters have sharper images because more dots were used to create them.

VP/TABS

This program—also from The Laser Edge—converts Lotus 1-2-3 spreadsheets into Ventura without editing. This utility works quickly and thoroughly. If you import Lotus 1-2-3 spreadsheets, this program should be part of your desktop publishing system.

VP/BASE

VP/BASE will simplify the task of publishing directories from your dBASE files. After creating a sample page of your directory in Ventura, VP/BASE analyzes its format and writes its own dBASE program to withdraw the data, tag it, and prepare it for importing into Ventura. The time it takes to master this program is well spent.

VPTOOLBOX

As you know, Ventura uses many different files to create a document. When you open a chapter, Ventura loads different text files, graphics files, a style sheet, and any other files used to create the document. Before long, keeping track of the files can become difficult.

VPToolbox takes the work out of managing files. This utility clearly displays the component files of any Ventura chapter. You can print this information for a permanent record and copy or delete the component files.

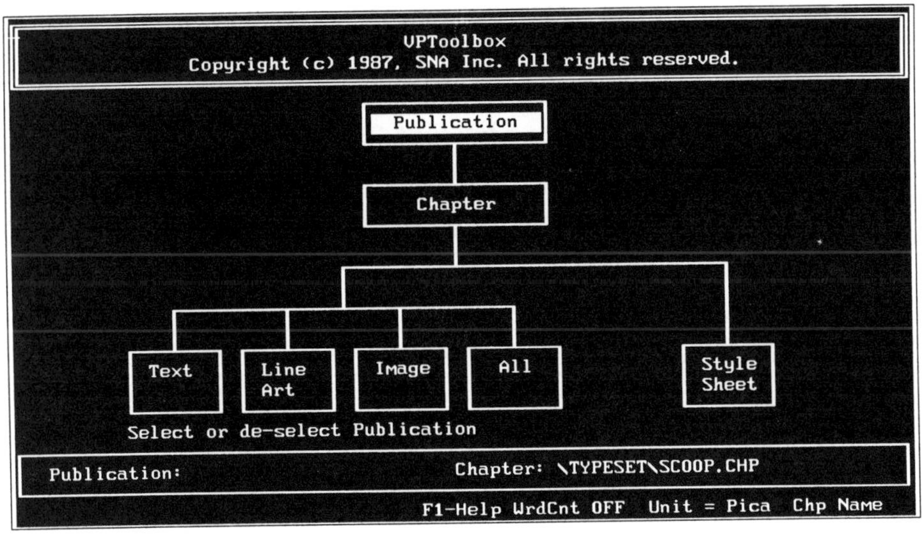

This figure illustrates a screen created by VPToolbox. This particular screen displays the component files of any Venutura chapter.

Figure 16.1

VPToolbox has another powerful feature: it shows you the components of a style sheet and allows you to print that information. Without VPToolbox, you cannot tell the contents of a style sheet without loading it.

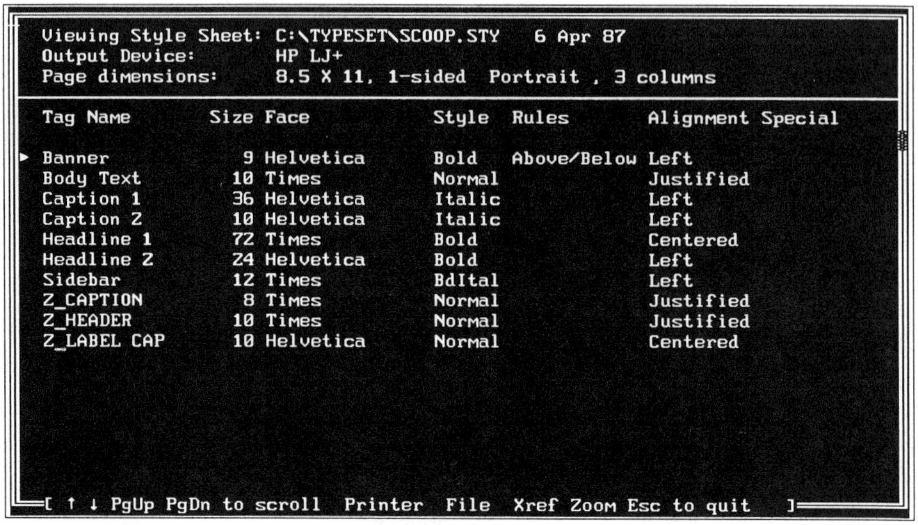

This VPToolbox screen displays the components of a particular Ventura style sheet.

Figure 16.2

VPToolbox can also help you import Lotus 1-2-3 style sheets and convert your text quotes to typeset quotes.

TABLE MANNERS

Although it is copy-protected, Table Manners is another utility program designed to help you import Lotus 1-2-3 spreadsheets.

EDCO HYPHENATION DICTIONARY

Adding a 130,000-word hyphenation dictionary to Ventura will improve text hyphenation. The actual Ventura dictionary is not a dictionary but a set of rules to help determine the appropriate place to hyphenate words. These rules do not always produce correct results. A two-megabyte memory board is required, so you may need to add extra memory. Of course, if you add additional memory, you can use it for other applications as well.

The hyphenation dictionary remains in computer memory, eliminating the need for disk access. (Excessive disk access during hyphenation slows Ventura's performance.)

If you are working with large texts – particularly with many columns – you should consider adding the EDCO Hyphenation Dictionary.

PUBSET

You may have access to – or will be connecting Ventura directly to – a typesetter instead of a laser printer. If you do, you will need a program to convert Ventura codes to typesetting codes. PubSet – also from EDCO – can do the job.

In addition to connecting Ventura to the Linotype typesetters, PubSet also allows you to directly connect Ventura to Compugraphic or Alphatype typesetting equipment. Pubset is a menu-driven program and is required to directly connect Ventura to true commercial typesetting equipment.

CHAPTER 17

WHERE TO FIND HELP

DESKTOP PUBLISHING RESOURCES

There are a variety of sources for additional desktop publishing information.

For help with operating Ventura, the following book—also published by MIS:Press—is an indispensable guide:

Ventura, by Rob Krumm
$21.95
ISBN 0-943518-37-7
MIS: Press
1107 N.W. 14th Avenue
Portland, OR 97209-2802
1-800-MANUALS

For more information about being a desktop publisher, the following source is valuable:

National Association of Desktop Publishers
P.O. Box 508
Kenmore Station
Boston, MA 02215-9998
(617) 437-6472

Monthly PC-based desktop publishing publications include the following:

Publish!
501 Second Street
San Francisco, CA 94107

Personal Publishing
25W550 Geneva Road
Wheaton, IL 60188

Electronic Publishing & Printing
650 Clark Street
Chicago, IL 60605

If you need technical help with Ventura, you can call the following Ventura support hotline number:

(214) 436-2616

For general publishing information, buy a copy of *The Complete Guide to Self-Publishing*. Published by Writer's Digest Books, this book offers tips on marketing, production, advertising, and promotion. It also offers advice on business matters, such as obtaining an ISBN and pricing your book.

The Complete Guide to Self Publishing
$19.95
ISBN 0-89879-167-7
Writer's Digest Books
1507 Dana Avenue
Cincinnati, OH 45207
(800) 543-4644

The following three magazines contain advice for magazine publishers:

Folio
P. O. Box 4006
New Canaan, CT 06840

Magazine Design and Production
4551 West 107th Street # 343
Overland, KS 66207

Small Press
R.R. Bowker Company
205 East 42nd Street
New York, NY 10017

Several local Ventura user groups have been established throughout the country. To find out if there is one near you, call your local Ventura dealer.

You can also contact (and join) the nationwide users group (VPUG) by calling (408) 778-1125 or by writing to the following address:

Ventura Publisher Users Group
16160 Caputo Drive
Morgan Hill, CA 95037

Throughout this book, different products have been mentioned, recommended, or discussed. Following is a list of products and manufacturers' names, addresses, and phone numbers. Contact individual companies for additional information.

PRODUCT DIRECTORY

Hardware

Product	**Manufacturer**
COMPAQ 386/20	Compaq Corporation 20555 FM 149 Houston, TX 77070 (713) 370-0670
Dest PC Scan 2000	DEST Corporation 1201 Cadillac Court Milpitas, CA 95035 (408) 946-7100
Gammafax	Gammalink 2452 Embarcadero Way Palo Alto, CA 94303 (415) 856-7421

Product	Manufacturer
HP LaserJet SeriesII	Hewlett-Packard 1820 Embarcadero Road Palo Alto, CA 94303 (800) 367-4772
LaserMaster CAPCard	LaserMaster Corp. P.O. Box 1439 Minnetonka, MN 55345 (612) 944-6069
Princeton LM 300 & LM 301 Big Screen Monitor	Princeton Graphic Systems 601 Ewing Street, Bldg. A Princeton, NJ 08540 (609) 683-1660
Publisher's Imagemaker	DP-Tek, Inc. P.O. Box 2411 Wichita, KS 67201 (316) 269-3068
QMS-PS-810 Laser Printer QMS Jet Script	QMS, Inc. One Magnum Pass Mobile, AL 36618 (205) 633-4300
Snap Shot	BioScan, Inc. 4520 Union Bay Place N.E. Seattle, WA 98105 (206) 523-5000
Viking Color Monitor	Moniterm Corp. 5740 Green Circle Drive Minnetonka, MN 55343 (612) 935-4151

Software

Product	Manufacturer
EDCO Hyphenation Dictionary & PubSet	EDCO Services, Inc. 12410 North Dale Mabry Hwy. Tampa, FL 33618 (813) 962-7800
ENERGRAPHICS	Enertronics Research, Inc. #5 Station Plaza 1910 Pine Street St. Louis, MO 63103 (314) 421-2771
Fontware	Bitstream Inc. Athenaeum House 215 First Street Cambridge, MA 02142 (617) 497-6222
GEM Presentation Team	Digital Research, Inc. Box DRI Monterey, CA 93942 (408) 649-3896
Grammatik II	Reference Software, Inc. 330 Townsend #131 San Francisco, CA 94017 (415) 541-0222
Headliner & Off The Wall	The Salinon Corporation P.O. Box 31047 Dallas, TX 75231 (214) 692-9091
HotShot	Symsoft 444 First Street., Ste K Los Altos, CA 94022 (415) 941-1552

Product	Manufacturer
Logitech Mouse	Logitech, Inc. 6505 Kaiser Drive Fremont, CA 94555 (415) 795-8500
Microsoft Word, Microsoft Mouse, and Microsoft Windows	Microsoft Corp. P.O. Box 97017 Redmond, WA 98073 (206) 882-8080
Norton Utilities 4.0 & Advanced Edition	Peter Norton Computing, Inc. 2210 Wilshire Blvd. Santa Monica, CA 90403 (213) 453-2361
PC PaintBrush Plus, and Publisher's Paintbrush	ZSoft Corp. 450 Franklin Rd., Ste.100 Marietta, GA 30067 (404) 428-0008
Publisher's PicturePak	Marketing Graphics Inc. 401 East Main Street Richmond, VA 23219 (804) 788-8844
RightWriter	Rightsoft, Inc. 2033 Wood Street #218 Sarasota, FL 33577 (813) 952-9211
SideKick & SuperKey	Borland International 4585 Scotts Valley Drive Scotts Valley, CA 95066 (408) 438-8400
TABLE MANNERS	The Desktop Publishing Group, Inc. 978 Douglas Avenue Suite 104 Alamonte Springs, FL 32714 (305) 682-4050

Product	Manufacturer
Ventura Publisher	Xerox Corp. P.O. Box 24 Rochester, NY 14692 (800) 832-6979
VP/SADDLE, VP/TABS, VP/BASE, & VP/FONTS	The Laser Edge 360-17th Street, Suite 203 Oakland, CA 94612 (415) 835-1581
VPToolbox	SNA, Inc. P.O. Box 3662 Princeton, NJ 08543 (609)683-1237
WordforWord	Mastersoft, Inc. 4621 N. 16th Street Phoenix, AZ 85016 (800) 624-6107
WordPerfect	WordPerfect Corp. 1555 N. Technology Way Orem, UT 84057 (801) 227-4010
WordStar	MicroPro Int'l Corp. 33 San Pablo Ave. San Rafael, CA 94903 (800) 227-5609

APPENDICES

APPENDIX A: VENTURA PUBLISHER STYLE SHEET CONTROL FORM

Page Description

Page Layout

```
     Orientation:  [] Portrait     [] Landscape

Paper Type:

     [] Half (5.5 x 8.5 in.)       [] Letter (8.5 x 11 in.)
     [] Legal (.5 x 14 in.)        [] Double (11 x 17 in.)
     [] B5 (17.6 x 25 cm.)         [] A4 (21 x 29.7 cm.)
     [] Broad Sheet (18 x 24 in.)

Sides:     [] Single          [] Double
Start On:  [] Left Side       [] Right Side
Kerning:   [] Globally On     [] Globally Off
```

Widows & Orphans

```
Minimum Isolated Lines at Top: []1  []2  []3  []4  []5
Minimum Isolated Lines at Bottom: []1  []2  []3  []4  []5
```

----

continued...

Auto-Numbering

[] On [] Off

Level 1:____
Level 2:____
Level 3:____
Level 4:____
Level 5:____
Level 6:____
Level 7:____
Level 8:____
Level 9:____
Level 10:____

Inserts: []Chapter # []1,2 []A,B []a,b []I,II []i,ii

Text Attributes:______________________________________

Headers & Footers

Left Page Header: [] On [] Off

Left:____
Center:____
Right:____

Inserts: []Chapter# []Page# []1st Match []Last Match

Text Attributes:____

Right Page Header: [] On [] Off

Left:____
Center:____
Right:____

Inserts: []Chapter# []Page# []1st Match []Last Match

Text Attributes:____

Left Page Footer: [] On [] Off

Left:____
Center:____
Right:____

Inserts: []Chapter# []Page# []1st Match []Last Match

Text Attributes:____

Right Page Footer [] On [] Off

Left:____
Center:____
Right:____

Inserts: []Chapter# []Page# []1st Match []Last Match

Text Attributes:____

Footnote Settings

[] Off [] Numbers From Start of Page (1, 2, 3)
[] Numbers From Start of Page (User-Defined)
[] Numbers From Start of Chapter (1, 2, 3)

Start With #:______ Number Template:___

Position of Number: []No Shift []Superscript []Subscript

User-Defined Strings: 1: *___ 2:**___ 3:***___ 4:****

5:+___ 6:++___ 7:+++___ 8:++++

Separator Line Width: ____.___ fractional points
Space Above Line: _________ Height of Line: _________

----

continued...

Frame Settings

Margins & Columns

```
Number of Columns:            []1 []2 []3 []4 []5 []6 []7 []8
Measurements expressed in:    []inches []cm [] picas & points

Left Page:     Column 1:  Width:__________
               Column 2:  Width:__________   Gutter:_________
               Column 3:  Width:__________   Gutter:________
               Column 4:  Width:__________   Gutter:_________
               Column 5:  Width:__________   Gutter:_________
               Column 6:  Width:__________   Gutter:_________
               Column 7:  Width:__________   Gutter:_________
               Column 8:  Width:__________   Gutter:_________

Right Page:    Column 1:  Width:__________
               Column 2:  Width:__________   Gutter:_________
               Column 3:  Width:__________   Gutter:_________
               Column 4:  Width:__________   Gutter:_________
               Column 5:  Width:__________   Gutter:_________
               Column 6:  Width:__________   Gutter:_________
               Column 7:  Width:__________   Gutter:_________
               Column 8:  Width:__________   Gutter:_________

Margins: Top:________ Bottom:________ Left:_______ Right:_______

-----------------------------------------------------------------
```

Sizing & Scaling

```
Upper Left X: ________ []+ []-

Upper Left Y: ________ []+ []-

Frame Width: _________                 Frame height:________

Horizontal Padding:____________        Vertical Padding: _____________

Picture Scaling:     []Fit in Frame []By Scale Factors
Aspect Ratio:        []Maintained   []By Scale Factors
Column Balance:      []On           []Off

-----------------------------------------------------------------
```

Vertical Rules

```
Measurements expressed in: []inches []cm [] picas & points

Left Page: Inter-Col. Rules Width: ________________________

Rule 1 Position: _____________   Rule 1 Width: _____________
Rule 2 Position: _____________   Rule 2 Width: _____________

Right Page: Inter-Col. Rules Width: ________________________

Rule 1 Position: _____________   Rule 1 Width: _____________
Rule 2 Position: _____________   Rule 2 Width: _____________

----------------------------------------------------------------
```

Ruling Lines Above

```
Measurements expressed in: []inches []cm [] picas & points

Width:     []None []Text []Margin []Column []Frame []Custom
Color:     []White[]Black[]Red[]Green []Blue []Cyan []Yellow[]Magenta
Pattern:   []1 []2 []3 []4 []5 []6 []7 []7 []Solid  []Dashes Off

Space Above Rule 1:________ Dash Width:___________
Height of Rule 1:__________ Dash Spacing:_________
Space Below Rule 1:________ Custom Indent:________
Height of Rule 2:__________ Custom Width:_________
Space Below Rule 2:________
Height of Rule 3:__________
Space Below Rule 3:________ []+ []-
Overall height:____________
Ruling Line Below

-------------------------------------------------------------------
```

continued...

```
Measurements expressed in: []inches []cm [] picas & points

Width:     []None []Text []Margin []Column []Frame []Custom
Color:     []White[]Black[]Red[]Green []Blue []Cyan []Yellow[]Magenta
Pattern:   []1 []2 []3 []4 []5 []6 []7 []7 []Solid  []Dashes Off

Space Above Rule 1:________ Dash Width:___________
Height of Rule 1:__________ Dash Spacing:_________
Space Below Rule 1:________ Custom Indent:________
Height of Rule 2:__________ Custom Width:_________
Space Below Rule 2:________
Height of Rule 3:__________
Space Below Rule 3:________ []+ []-
Overall height:____________

----------------------------------------------------------------
```

Ruling Box Around

```
Measurements expressed in: []inches []cm [] picas & points

Width:     []None []Text []Margin []Column []Frame []Custom
Color:     []White[]Black[]Red[]Green []Blue []Cyan []Yellow[]Magenta
Pattern:   []1 []2 []3 []4 []5 []6 []7 []7 []Solid  []Dashes Off

Space Above Rule 1:________ Dash Width:___________
Height of Rule 1:__________ Dash Spacing:_________
Space Below Rule 1:________ Custom Indent:________
Height of Rule 2:__________ Custom Width:_________
Space Below Rule 2:________
Height of Rule 3:__________
Space Below Rule 3:________ []+ []-
Overall height:____________

----------------------------------------------------------------
```

Frame Background

```
Color:     []White[]Black[]Red[]Green []Blue []Cyan []Yellow[]Magenta
Pattern:   []1 []2 []3 []4 []5 []6 []7 []7 []Solid  []Hollow

----------------------------------------------------------------
```

Paragraph Tags

Tag Name:____________________

Font

Font____________Face____________Size____________Style__________

Color: []White[]Black[]Red[]Green []Blue []Cyan []Yellow[]Magenta

---

Alignment

Alignment: []Left []Center []Right []Justified
Hyphenation: []Off []USEnglish []Spanish
Successive Hyphens: []1 []2 []3 []4 []5 []Unlimited
Width: []Column-Wide []Frame-Wide
First Line: []Indent []Outdent

In/Outdent Width:_____picas & points
In/Outdent Height:_______lines

Relative Indent: []None []Length of Previous Line

Spacing

Above:_________Below:_________
Inter-line:_____Inter-paragraph:________

Add in Above: []Always []When not At Column Top

Left Page: In From Left:______ In From Right:_______
Right Page:In From Left:______ In From Right:_______

---

continued...

Breaks

Page Break: []No []Before []After Before & After
[]Before/Until Left []Before/Until Right

Column Break:[]No []Before []After [] Before & After

Line Break:[]No []Before []After [] Before & After

Next Y Position: []Normal []Beside Last Line of Prev. Paragraph

Allow Within: []Yes []No Keep With Next: []Yes []No

Tabs

Type: []Off []Left []Center []Right []Decimal
Display: []Shown as Open Space []Shown as Leader Char
Location: _________ Leader Char: []Spaces []... []_ []Other____
Leader Spacing: []0 []1 []2 []3 []4 []5 []6 []7 []8

Special Effects: []None []Big First Character []Bullet
Font____________Face____________Size____________Style___________

Color: []White[]Black[]Red[]Green []Blue []Cyan []Yellow[]Magenta
Space for Big First Character: []Normal []Custom

Show Bullet As: ________Bullet Character:________(ASCII)
Indent After Bullet:____________

Typographic Controls

```
Automatic Kerning: []Off []On
Letter Spacing: []Off []On  Up to __Ems
Tracking:_____Ems []Looser []Tighter

Minimum Space Width:__________
Normal Space Width: __________
Maximum Space Width:__________
Overscore Height:  ___________  Shift Up By:________
Strike-Thru Height:___________  Shift Up By:________
Underline 1 Height:___________  Shift Down By:______
Underline 2 Height:___________  Shift Down By:______
```

Ruling Lines Above

```
Measurements expressed in: []inches []cm [] picas & points

Width:    []None []Text []Margin []Column []Frame []Custom
Color:    []White[]Black[]Red[]Green []Blue []Cyan []Yellow[]Magenta
Pattern:  []1 []2 []3 []4 []5 []6 []7 []7 []Solid  []Dashes Off

Space Above Rule 1:________ Dash Width:___________
Height of Rule 1:__________ Dash Spacing:_________
Space Below Rule 1:________ Custom Indent:________
Height of Rule 2:__________ Custom Width:_________
Space Below Rule 2:________
Height of Rule 3:__________
Space Below Rule 3:________ []+ []-
Overall height:____________
```

----

continued...

Ruling Lines Below

Measurements expressed in: []inches []cm [] picas & points

Width: []None []Text []Margin []Column []Frame []Custom
Color: []White[]Black[]Red[]Green []Blue []Cyan []Yellow[]Magenta
Pattern: []1 []2 []3 []4 []5 []6 []7 []7 []Solid []Dashes Off

Space Above Rule 1:________ Dash Width:___________
Height of Rule 1:__________ Dash Spacing:_________
Space Below Rule 1:________ Custom Indent:________
Height of Rule 2:__________ Custom Width:_________
Space Below Rule 2:________
Height of Rule 3:__________
Space Below Rule 3:________ []+ []-
Overall height:____________

APPENDIX B: THE JOLLIE MOLLIE REPORT

The Jollie Mollie Report has been frequently mentioned and used in illustrations throughout this book. This appendix contains the entire Jollie Mollie Report, from how it would appear as typewritten text to its final form created in Ventura Publisher.

The report was created using the following steps:

1. The text was written in WordPerfect 4.2.
2. The Lotus 1-2-3 spreadsheet and graph were created in Lotus 2.0.
3. The Energraphics 3-D graph was created in Energraphics 3.0.
4. The Ventura Style Sheet &BOOK-P1.STY was used, and additional tags were created as needed.
5. The Ruling Box Around option from the Paragraph menu was used for the imported pictures.
6. A header was added, using the Headers and Footers option from the Page menu.

The first illustration (Figure B.1) depicts how the Jollie Mollie Report would look if prepared on a typewriter.

ADVERTISING CAMPAIGN

THE JOLLIE MOLLIE PROMOTION

for

THE TWISTER PRETZELS SNACK

Prepared for the PENNSYLVANIA FOOD CORPORATION

AN OVERVIEW:

In April, a new snack food will be introduced and marketed by the Pennsylvania Food Corporation. This new product line, The Twister Pretzels Snack, will be extensively marketed nationwide. In order to kick off the campaign, an advertising and promotional strategy will be instituted. This report submits our conclusion and recommendation to use the Jollie Mollie Promotion.

TEST MARKETING RESULTS:

The Twister Pretzels Snack has been test marketed in Harrisburg, Pennsylvania, Atlanta, Georgia, Weatherford, Texas, and Las Vegas, Nevada. The results from consumer surveys have remained constant: The Twister Pretzel Snack is tasty and delicious. However, consumers stated repeatedly that although they would repurchase the product, the name recognition of the snack is unlikely to be retained. Accordingly, we feel repeat sales would diminish unless some sort of instant name recognition is developed and associated with The Twister Pretzel Snack.

We have considered various possible promotions. By an overall consensus of the evaluation committee in the Marketing Department, we firmly believe the Jollie Mollie Promotion is the strongest concept developed. We strongly recommend and urge the use of the Jollie Mollie Promotion to develop the name recognition we need for our new Twister Pretzel Snack product line.

THE JOLLIE MOLLIE PROMOTION

The Jollie Mollie Promotion consists of using a Boxer dog, named Jollie Mollie, as our advertising mascot. Jollie Mollie, the Boxer Dog, would rather eat a Twister Pretzel Snack, than her dog food. And she would do anything for a Twister Pretzel Snack, including the twister, a special dog dance where she twists and jumps with joy in the anticipation of eating a Twister Pretzel Snack.

Figure B.1 (continued on next page)

We see immense possibilities with an advertising campaign such as this. Cute animals have successively worked in the past in advertising promotions. We see no reason why the Jollie Mollie concept will not enjoy immense, and instant acceptance by the public.

We see the Jollie Mollie advertising attracting public attention quickly. We recommend the use of Twister music, a spin off from the old Twist dance music. When ever the music starts, we will normally see a crowded room, in a party atmosphere. In the center of the happy group will be Jollie Mollie, doing her Twist in anticipation of the Twister Pretzel Snack.

POSSIBLE NEGATIVE CONCEPTS

We did express two concerns over using a dog in our campaign. We wanted to make certain that we received no adverse publicity for feeding a dog pretzels over its regular dog food. For that reason, we will never show Jollie Mollie actually eating a Twister Pretzel Snack. Secondly, we did not want our pretzels associated with dog food products. We believe by having people in our advertising actually eating and enjoying the product, this problem will be overcome. We also feel that by using the voice-over announcement at the end of each commercial saying, "Jollie Mollie will do the Twister for a Twister Pretzel Snack. What would you do for a Twister?" will prevent any misdirected product identification.

We also agreed that other companies, most notably a brewing company selling beer, used a dog successfully in their advertising campaigns. And in our research, we found no indication that anyone complained about a dog drinking alcoholic beverages. We did note, however, that some schools were complaining about the effectiveness of the advertising, and were fearful that the dog was promoting beer drinking among the young. We reiterate our belief that by using a dog as our lead in the promotion of the product, instant name recognition will be built.

THE JOLLIE MOLLIE LOGO

We feel there should be an all-out effort to promote Jollie Mollie. Personal appearances at retail stores, malls, and distributors throughout the nation, Jollie-Mollie T-Shirts and baseball caps (available through mail order and by using an order form on our package), the Jollie Mollie fan club, and even a contest, "What I'd do for a Twister!" should be started.

Figure B.1 (continued on next page)

We think the likeness of Jollie Mollie should be included on our package, on our trucks, and on all ad displays provided to the retailers.

We firmly believe that we can create a new national symbol, a new national image, and instant name recognition of the Twister Pretzel Snack.

ADDITIONAL INFORMATION:

Included with this report are sample scripts, for both TV advertising and radio spots, estimated costs for production, promotional plans for the personal appearances of Jollie Mollie, the establishment of the Jollie Mollie fan club, the results of the consumer studies and surveys, the report on other advertising campaigns considered, and why they were rejected. We have also attached other information, such as distribution costs, anticipated profits, costs of advertising, break even and profit margins.

Figure B.1

Figure B.2 demonstrates the proper method for preparing the text in word processor to be imported into Ventura. Note that the text may seem hard to read because double spaces between sentences and double carriage returns have been eliminated. Also, paragraph tags have been added.

```
@PARAFILTER ON =
@HEADLINE 1 = ADVERTISING CAMPAIGN
@HEADLINE 2 = THE JOLLIE MOLLIE PROMOTION
@B2 = for
@HEADLINE 1 = THE TWISTER PRETZELS SNACK
@HEADLINE 2 = Prepared for the PENNSYLVANIA FOOD COR]
@MINOR HEADING = AN OVERVIEW:
In April, a new snack food will be introduced and mar}
Pennsylvania Food Corporation. This new product lin
Pretzels Snack, will be extensively marketed nation
to kick off the campaign, an advertising and promoti
will be instituted. This report submits our conclus:
recommendation to use the Jollie Mollie Promotion.
@MINOR HEADING = TEST MARKETING RESULTS:
The Twister Pretzels Snack has been test marketed in
Pennsylvania, Atlanta, Georgia, Weatherford, Texas, and Las
Vegas, Nevada. The results from consumer surveys have remained
constant: The Twister Pretzel Snack is tasty and delicious.
However, consumers stated repeatedly that although they would
```

Figure B.2 (continued on next page)

repurchase the product, the name recognition of the snack is unlikely to be retained. Accordingly, we feel repeat sales would diminish unless some sort of instant name recognition is developed and associated with The Twister Pretzel Snack.
We have considered various possible promotions. By an overall consensus of the evaluation committee in the Marketing Department, we firmly believe the Jollie Mollie Promotion is the strongest concept developed. We strongly recommend and urge the use of the Jollie Mollie Promotion to develop the name recognition we need for our new Twister Pretzel Snack product line.
@MINOR HEADING = THE JOLLIE MOLLIE PROMOTION
The Jollie Mollie Promotion consists of using a Boxer dog, named Jollie Mollie, as our advertising mascot. Jollie Mollie, the Boxer Dog, would rather eat a Twister Pretzel Snack, than her dog food. And she would do anything for a Twister Pretzel Snack, including the twister, a special dog dance where she twists and jumps with joy in the anticipation of eating a Twister Pretzel Snack.
We see immense possibilities with an advertising campaign such as this. Cute animals have successively worked in the past in advertising promotions. We see no reason why the Jollie Mollie concept will not enjoy immense, and instant acceptance by the public.
We see the Jollie Mollie advertising attracting public attention quickly. We recommend the use of Twister music, a spin off from the old Twist dance music. When ever the music starts, we will normally see a crowded room, in a party atmosphere. In the center of the happy group will be Jollie Mollie, doing her Twist in anticipation of the Twister Pretzel Snack.
@MINOR HEADING = POSSIBLE NEGATIVE CONCEPTS
We did express two concerns over using a dog in our campaign. We wanted to make certain that we received no adverse publicity for feeding a dog pretzels over its regular dog food. For that reason, we will never show Jollie Mollie actually eating a Twister Pretzel Snack. Secondly, we did not want our pretzels associated with dog food products. We believe by having people in our advertising actually eating and enjoying the product, this problem will be overcome. We also feel that by using the voice-over announcement at the end of each commercial saying, "Jollie Mollie will do the Twister for a Twister Pretzel Snack. What would you do for a Twister?" will prevent any misdirected product identification.
We also agreed that other companies, most notably a brewing company selling beer, used a dog successfully in their advertising campaigns. And in our research, we found no indication that anyone complained about a dog drinking alcoholic

Figure B.2 (continued on next page)

beverages. We did note, however, that some schools were complaining about the effectiveness of the advertising, and were fearful that the dog was promoting beer drinking among the young. We reiterate our belief that by using a dog as our lead in the promotion of the product, instant name recognition will be built.
@MINOR HEADING = THE JOLLIE MOLLIE LOGO
We feel there should be an all-out effort to promote Jollie Mollie. Personal appearances at retail stores, malls, and distributors throughout the nation, Jollie-Mollie T-Shirts and baseball caps (available through mail order and by using an order form on our package), the Jollie Mollie fan club, and even a contest, "What I'd do for a Twister!" should be started.
We think the likeness of Jollie Mollie should be included on our package, on our trucks, and on all ad displays provided to the retailers.
We firmly believe that we can create a new national symbol, a new national image, and instant name recognition of the Twister Pretzel Snack.
@MINOR HEADING = ADDITIONAL INFORMATION:
Included with this report are sample scripts, for both TV advertising and radio spots, estimated costs for production, promotional plans for the personal appearances of Jollie Mollie, the establishment of the Jollie Mollie fan club, the results of the consumer studies and surveys, the report on other advertising campaigns considered, and why they were rejected. We have also attached other information, such as distribution costs, anticipated profits, costs of advertising, break even and profit margins.

Figure B.2

Finally, the complete Jollie Mollie Report, as produced in Ventura, is presented in Figure B.3. Note that the Lotus 1-2-3 spreadsheet data has been imported, as well as the Lotus 1-2-3 graph and the Energraphics three-dimensional graph.

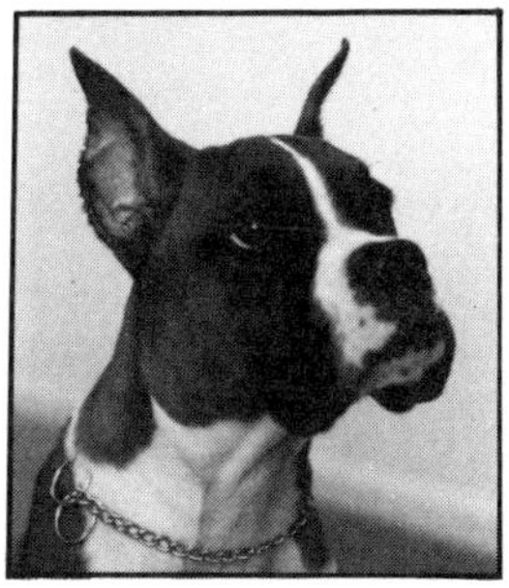

ADVERTISING CAMPAIGN

THE JOLLIE MOLLIE PROMOTION

for

THE TWISTER PRETZELS SNACK

Prepared for the
PENNSYLVANIA FOOD CORPORATION

AN OVERVIEW:

In April, a new snack food will be introduced and marketed by the Pennsylvania Food Corporation. This new product line, The Twister Pretzels Snack, will be extensively marketed nationwide. In order to kick off the campaign, an advertising and promotional strategy will be instituted. This report submits our conclusion and recommendation to use the Jollie Mollie Promotion.

Figure B.3 (continued on next page)

TEST MARKETING RESULTS:

The Twister Pretzels Snack has been test marketed in Harrisburg, Pennsylvania, Atlanta, Georgia, Weatherford, Texas, and

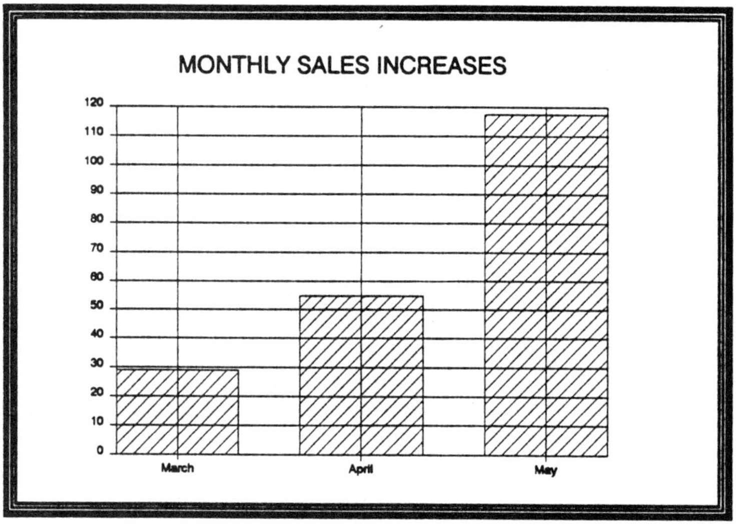

Las Vegas, Nevada. The results from consumer surveys have remained constant: The Twister Pretzel Snack is tasty and delicious. However, consumers stated repeatedly that although they would repurchase the product, the name recognition of the snack is unlikely to be retained. Accordingly, we feel repeat sales would diminish unless some sort of instant name recognition is developed and associated with The Twister Pretzel Snack.

We have considered various possible promotions. By an overall consensus of the evaluation committee in the Marketing Department, we firmly believe the Jollie Mollie Promotion is the strongest concept developed. We strongly recommend and urge the use of the Jollie Mollie Promotion to develop the name recognition we need for our new Twister Pretzel Snack product line.

Figure B.3 (continued on next page)

THE JOLLIE MOLLIE PROMOTION

The Jollie Mollie Promotion consists of using a Boxer dog, named Jollie Mollie, as our advertising mascot. Jollie Mollie, the Boxer Dog, would rather eat a Twister Pretzel Snack, than her dog food. And she would do anything for a Twister Pretzel Snack, including the twister, a special dog dance where she twists and jumps with joy in the anticipation of eating a Twister Pretzel Snack.

We see immense possibilities with an advertising campaign such as this. Cute animals have successively worked in the past in advertising promotions. We see no reason why the Jollie Mollie

Market	March	April	May
Harrisburg PA	$12,124.00	$22,870.00	$38,674.00
Atlanta GA	$5,434.00	$13,190.00	$34,234.00
Weatherford	$2,311.00	$7,609.00	$21,234.00
Las Vegas	$9,099.00	$11,108.00	$23,450.00
TOTAL	**$28,968.00**	**$54,777.00**	**$117,592.00**

Test Marketing Results

concept will not enjoy immense, and instant acceptance by the public.

We see the Jollie Mollie advertising attracting public attention quickly. We recommend the use of Twister music, a spin off from the old Twist dance music. Whenever the music starts, we will normally see a crowded room, in a party atmosphere. In the center of the happy group will be Jollie Mollie, doing her Twist in anticipation of the Twister Pretzel Snack.

Figure B.3 (continued on next page)

POSSIBLE NEGATIVE CONCEPTS

We did express two concerns over using a dog in our campaign. We wanted to make certain that we received no adverse publicity for feeding a dog pretzels over its regular dog food. For that reason, we will never show Jollie Mollie actually eating a Twister Pretzel Snack. Secondly, we did not want our pretzels associated

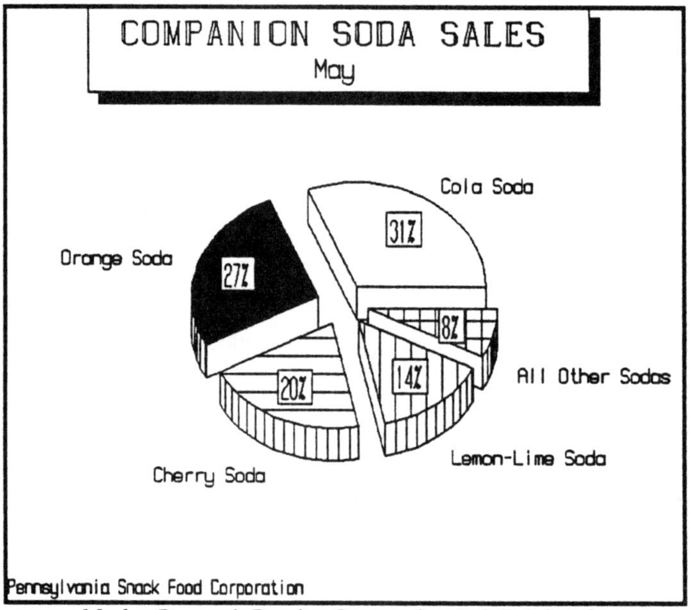

Market Research Results: Companion Soft Drink Sales

with dog food products. We believe by having people in our advertising actually eating and enjoying the product, this problem will be overcome. We also feel that by using the voice-over announcement at the end of each commercial saying, "Jollie Mollie will do the Twister for a Twister Pretzel Snack. What would you do for a Twister?" will prevent any misdirected product identification.

We also agreed that other companies, most notably a brewing company selling beer, used a dog successfully in their advertising campaigns. And in our research, we found no indication that

Figure B.3 (continued on next page)

anyone complained about a dog drinking alcoholic beverages. We did note, however, that some schools were complaining about the effectiveness of the advertising, and were fearful that the dog was promoting beer drinking among the young. We reiterate our belief that by using a dog as our lead in the promotion of the product, instant name recognition will be built.

THE JOLLIE MOLLIE LOGO

We feel there should be an all-out effort to promote Jollie Mollie. Personal appearances at retail stores, malls, and distributors throughout the nation, Jollie-Mollie T-Shirts and baseball caps (available through mail order and by using an order form on our package), the Jollie Mollie fan club, and even a contest, "What I'd do for a Twister!" should be started.

We think the likeness of Jollie Mollie should be included on our package, on our trucks, and on all ad displays provided to the retailers.

We firmly believe that we can create a new national symbol, a new national image, and instant name recognition of the Twister Pretzel Snack.

ADDITIONAL INFORMATION:

Included with this report are sample scripts, for both TV advertising and radio spots, estimated costs for production, promotional plans for the personal appearances of Jollie Mollie, the establishment of the Jollie Mollie fan club, the results of the consumer studies and surveys, the report on other advertising campaigns considered, and why they were rejected. We have also attached other information, such as distribution costs, anticipated profits, costs of advertising, break even and profit

Figure B.3

APPENDIX C: LOGOS

A trademark is a logo that immediately identifies the company or product. Many logos have become familiar because they are constantly used in advertisements. McDonald's has its golden arches. Coca-Cola has its Coke emblem. IBM has its letters created with lines. Proctor & Gamble has its moon. General Motors has its Chevy emblem. Logos are used to enhance a company's image.

This appendix contains many different examples of how a logo was incorporated into designs for the fictitious Pennsylvania Snack Food Corporation. The logo is actually a piece of clip art from Marketing Graphics Incorporated Publisher's PicturePak, the Eye Openers—Executive & Management Edition.

Clip art purchased from Marketing Graphics Incorporated, as well as other sources, is copyrighted. Accordingly, you cannot copyright the clip art. In the license agreement provided with the software, you are usually granted the use of the clip art for any purpose other than reselling or distributing the pictures as clip art. You probably should not use a piece of clip art as a trademark because others could use it, and you could not register it as your own work.

However, you can use clip art as the starting point for a logo. You can use your paint and draw program to enhance the appearance of a piece of clip art by rotating, filling, adding, or reversing the image.

In these examples, the author used a simple design of an arrow, and, after working with it, positioned it in various ways to create different designs and products.

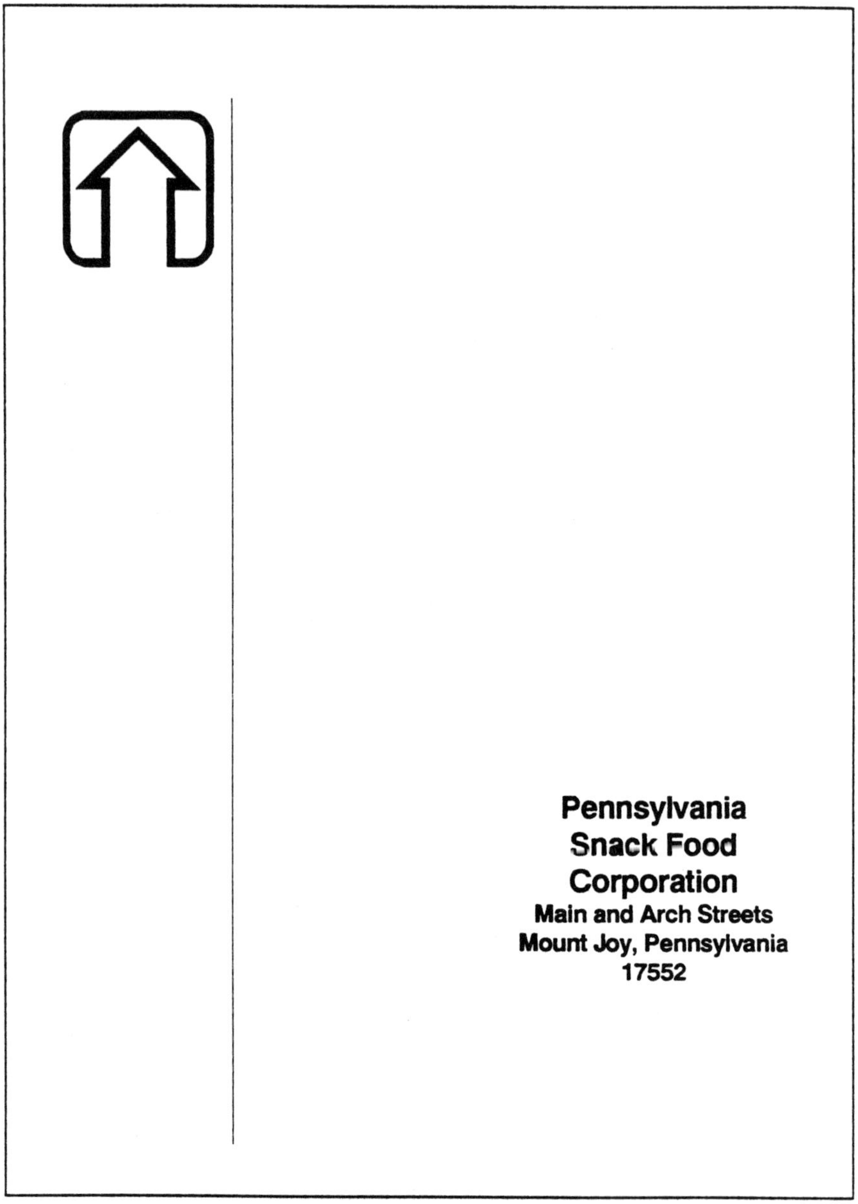

A report cover for the Jollie Mollie advertising campaign. In this simple design, a rule separates the company's name and the logo. Notice the clean look created by using white space. Sans-serif type (Ventura's Swiss) was used. This typeface offers a clean, bold image.

Figure C.1

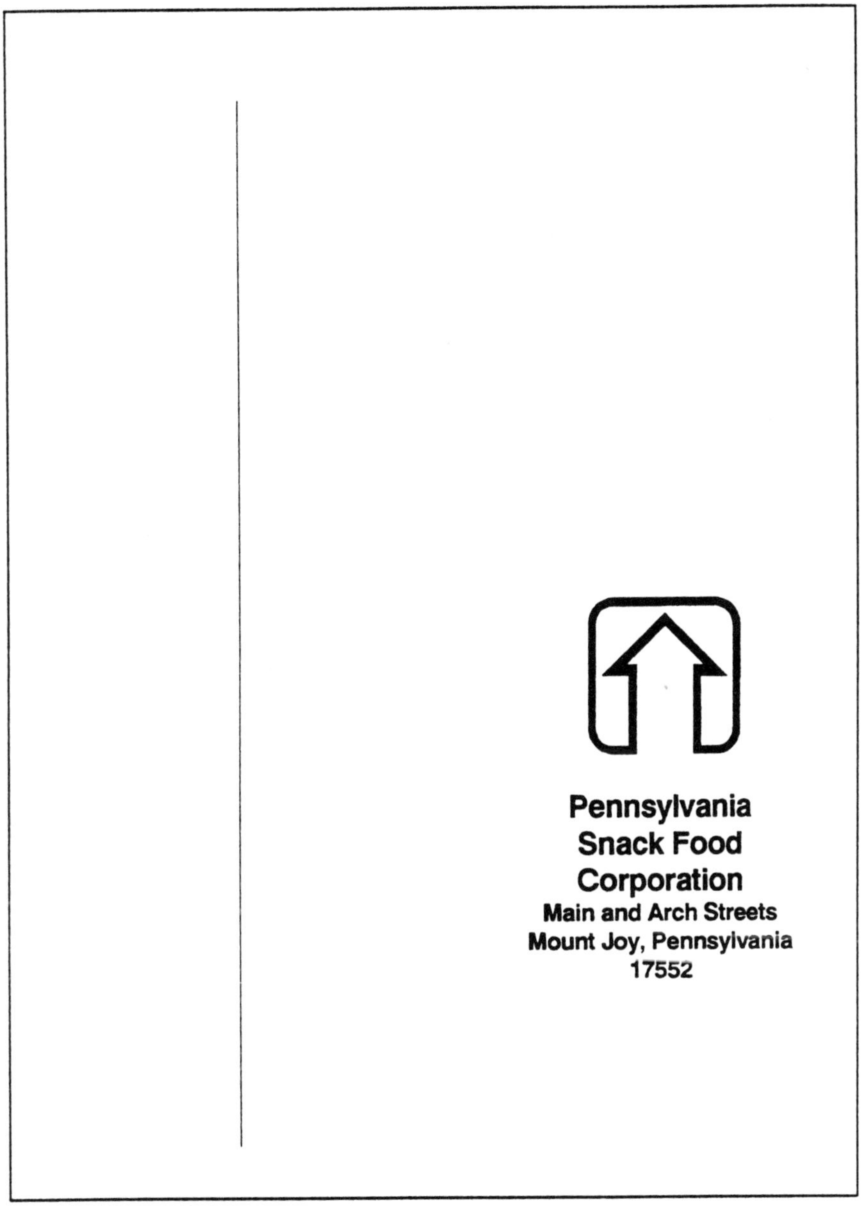

In another report cover design, the logo is moved to the text area. The reader's eye is drawn immediately to the logo and company name.

Figure C.2

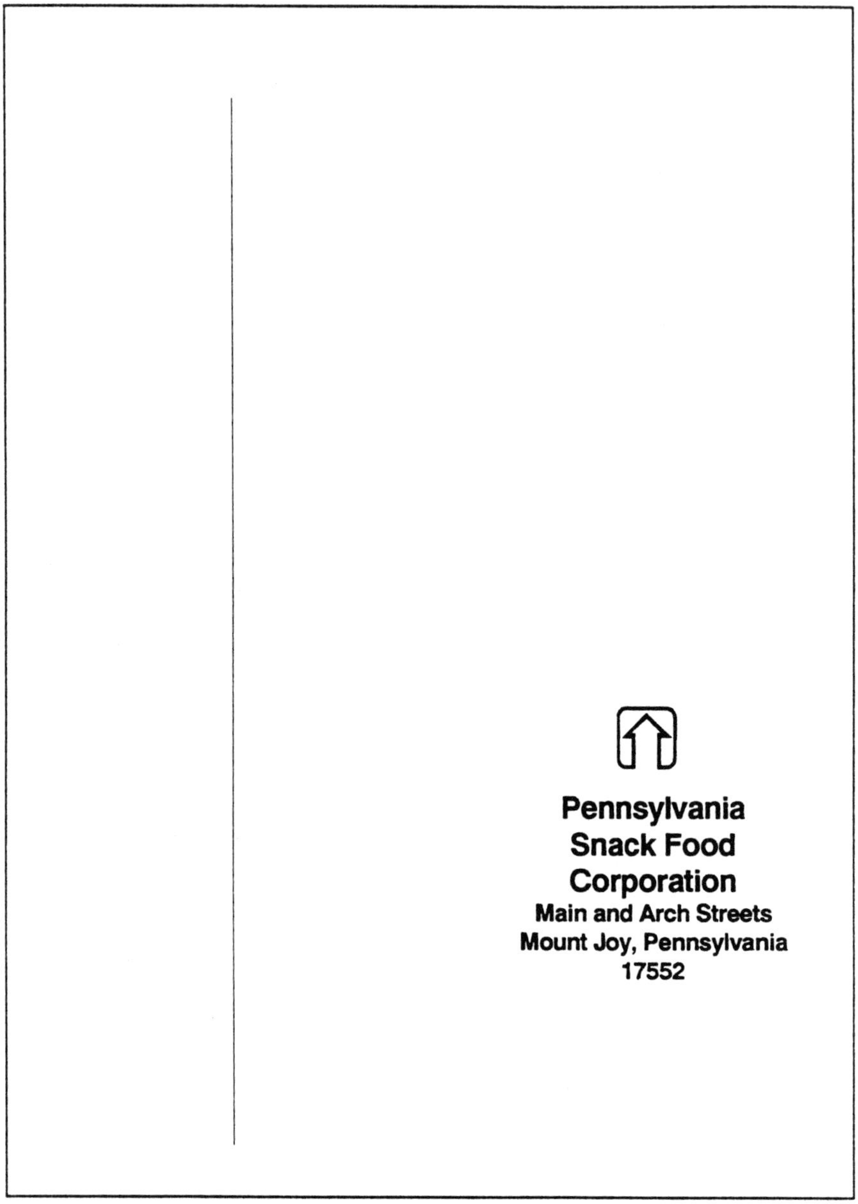

Similar to the example in Figure C.2, in this example, the logo has been reduced. Compare the difference between this illustration and Figure C.2. Notice how the larger logo immediately catches your eye in Figure C.2; however, in Figure C.3, the bold type also catches your eye, and you are more likely to read the words than to first notice the logo. This design also offers a clean look with an effective use of white space.

Figure C.3

Pennsylvania Snack Food Corporation

Main and Arch Streets
Mount Joy, PA 17552

This is a simple, basic design. It may seem bland at first because this concept has been used so often; however, it is used so often because it is a solid design concept. The page elements – the type and the logo – are balanced.

Figure C.4

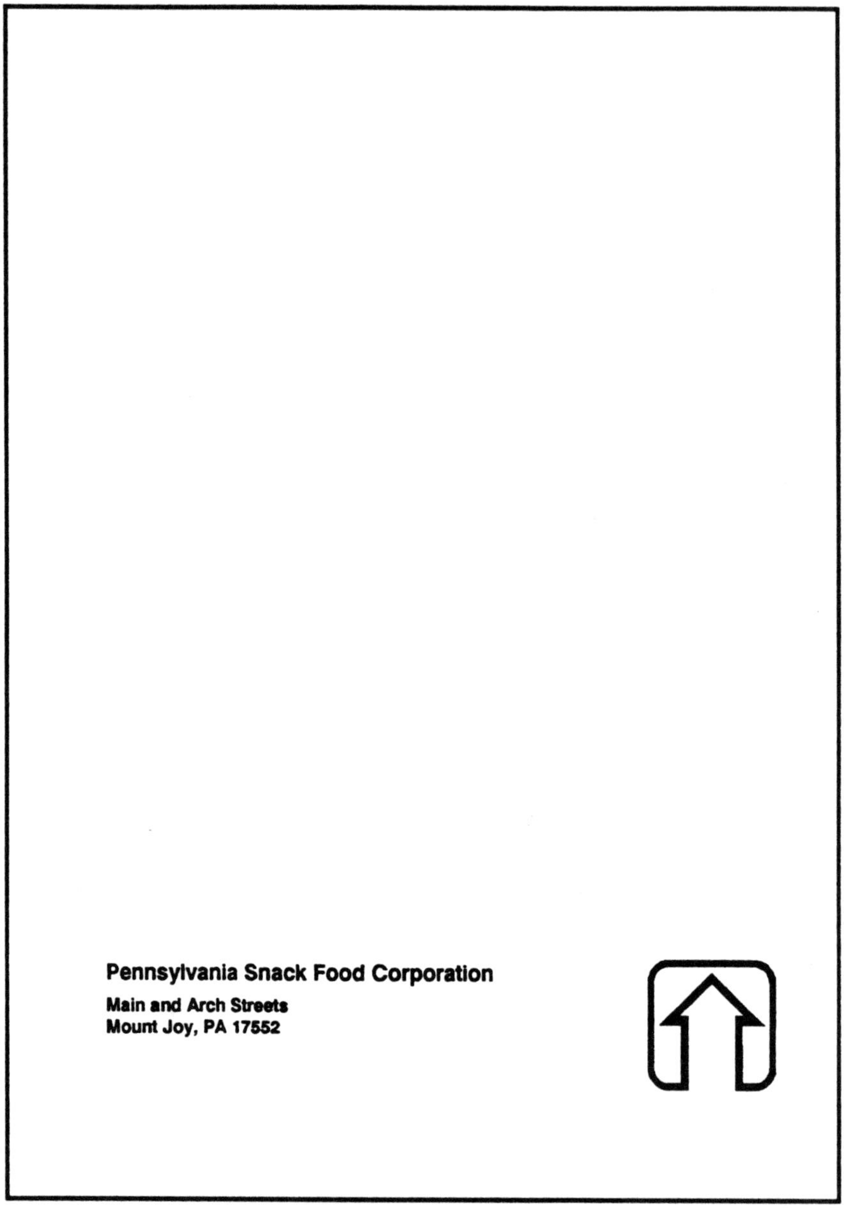

Note the use of white space in this design. Here, the report cover does not contain a vertical rule. Compare this example to Figures C.1, C.2, and C.3. Because this book is bound, your eye will naturally be drawn to the outer edge of the unbound side of the page.

Figure C.5

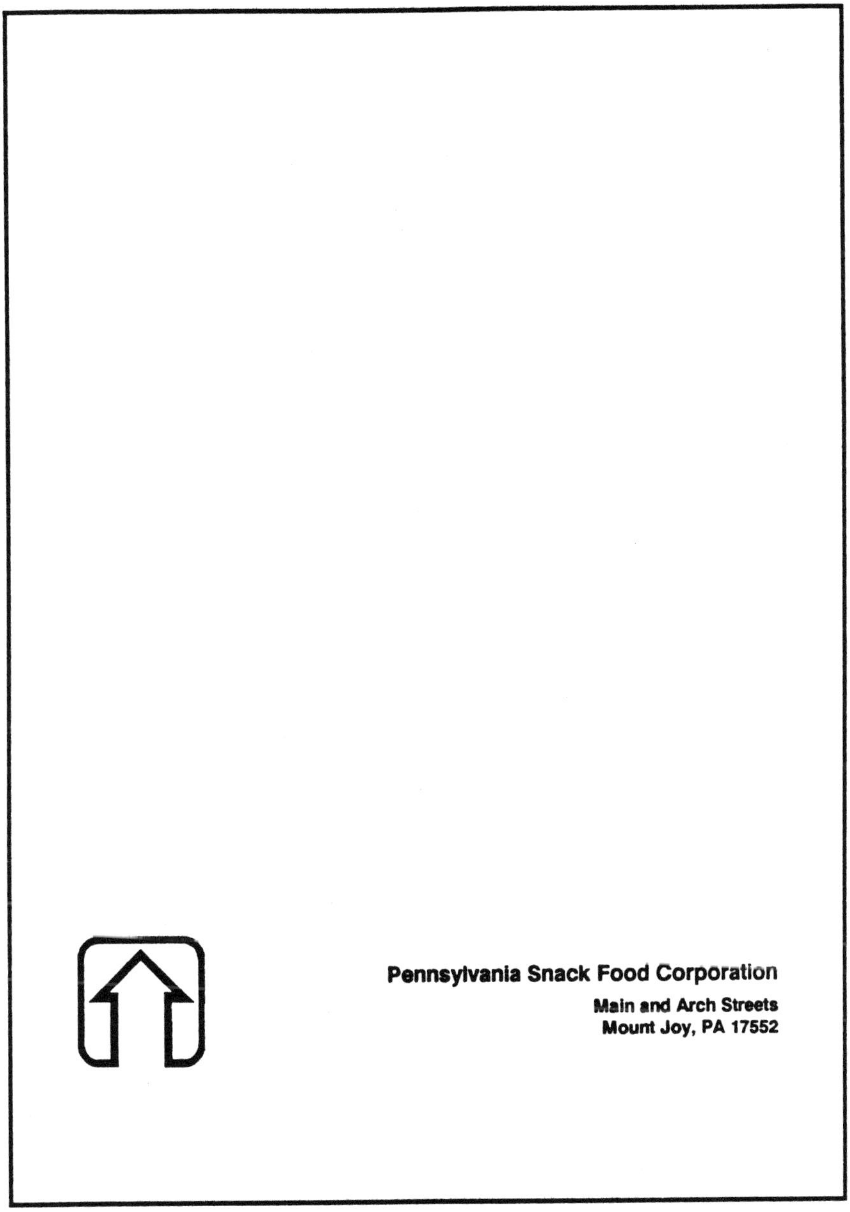

This example is very similar to Figure C.5, but compare the two. When you examine these examples, what do you see first—the logo or the company name? You should naturally notice the element on the outer, unbound edge, so whichever you want to emphasize—the logo or the company name—should be positioned on the outer, unbound edge.

Figure C.6

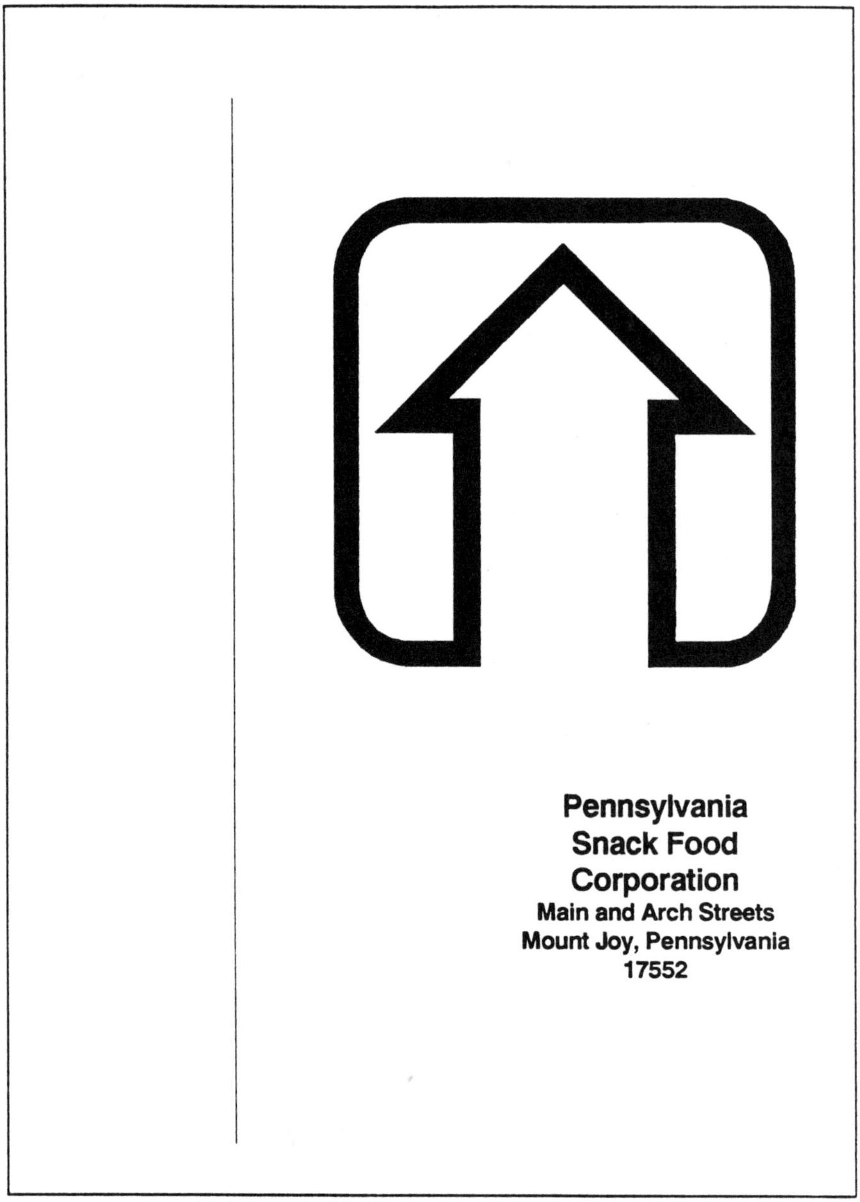

In this example, the logo's size has been greatly increased. It certainly overpowers the type. Logos, which are supposed to be easily recognized, are one design element that can be used in an overpowering manner.

Figure C.7

Pennsylvania Snack Food Corporation

Main and Arch Streets
Mount Joy, Pennsylvania 17552

This logo is stretched out of shape by using Ventura's Sizing & Scaling option, which is selected from the Frame Menu. The Picture Scaling option was set to Fit in Frame and the Aspect Ratio option set to Distorted. This is the result. Because logos represent a company's image, you do not want to distort it, or make it appear different from one document to another.

Figure C.8

Pennsylvania Snack
Food Corporation
Main and Arch Streets
Mount Joy, PA 17552

In this design, the text was placed within the logo. Only your taste and opinion can determine whether you like this design.

Figure C.9

Pennsylvania Snack Food Corporation

Main and Arch Streets
Mount Joy, Pennsylvania 17552

Letterheads can also be created using Ventura. In this example, all elements are placed at the top of the page.

Figure C.10

Pennsylvania Snack Food Corporation
Main and Arch Streets   Mount Joy, Pennsylvania 17552

Compare this example to Figure C.10. The logo is smaller. The type occupies only two lines instead of three. It takes up less overall space on the page.

Figure C.11

The letterhead design can be used with a business card and an envelope.

Figure C.12

Pennsylvania Snack Food Corporation

Main and Arch Streets
Mount Joy, Pennsylvania 17552

To present a different image, a background was added to the frame containing the logo.

Figure C.13

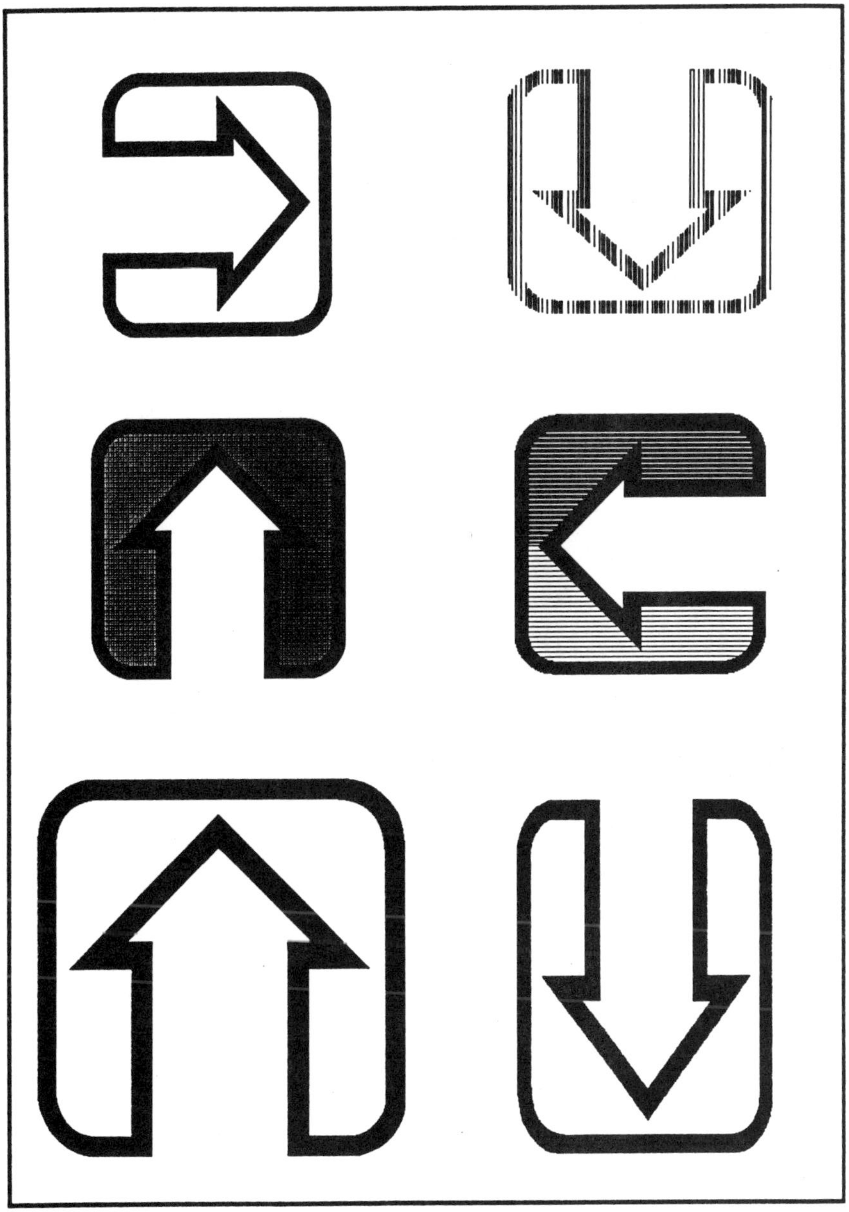

Using ZSoft's Publisher's Paintbrush, the logo has been rotated, filled, resized, and reversed. By using this or another paint-and-draw program, you can add impact to your logos or simply change their appearance. Each of the examples in this appendix has been created and modified using Publisher's Paintbrush.

Figure C.14

APPENDIX D: FRAMES

You can create many special effects using Ventura Publisher frames. This appendix includes examples of special images created with Ventura frames.

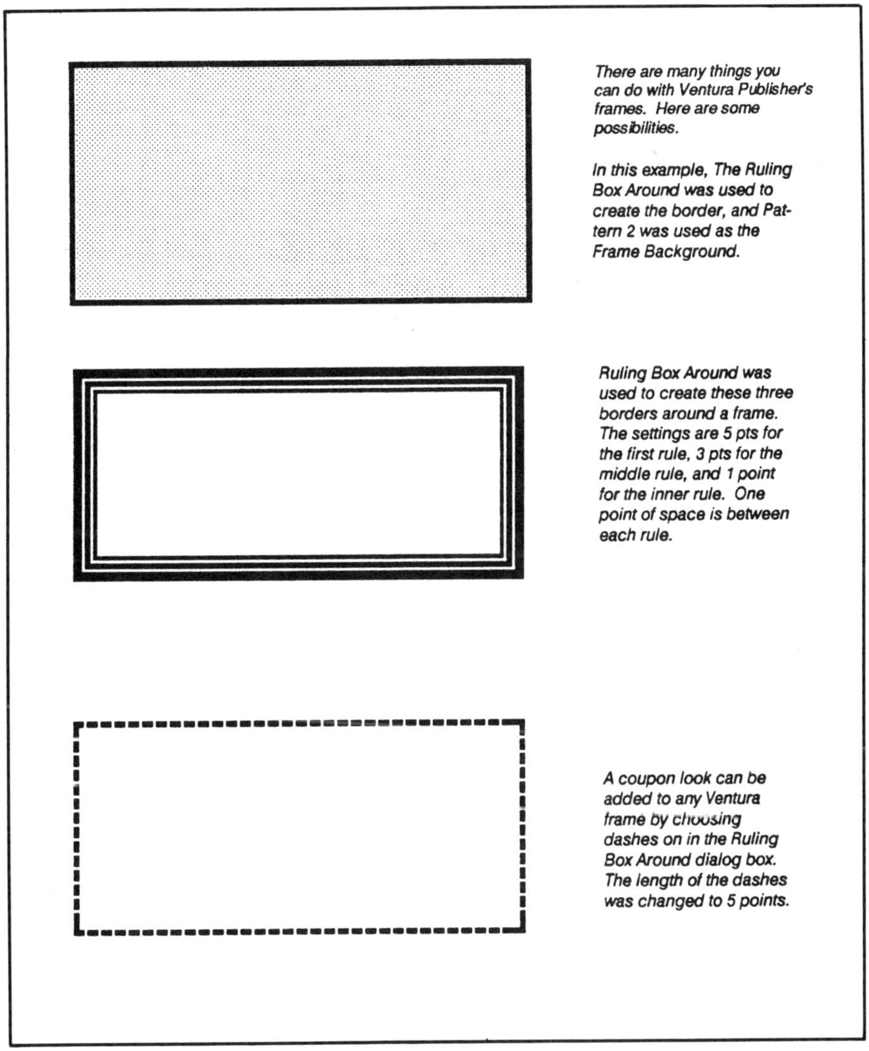

There are many things you can do with Ventura Publisher's frames. Here are some possibilities.

In this example, The Ruling Box Around was used to create the border, and Pattern 2 was used as the Frame Background.

Ruling Box Around was used to create these three borders around a frame. The settings are 5 pts for the first rule, 3 pts for the middle rule, and 1 point for the inner rule. One point of space is between each rule.

A coupon look can be added to any Ventura frame by choosing dashes on in the Ruling Box Around dialog box. The length of the dashes was changed to 5 points.

You can create frames with various appearances in your document, just by experimenting with the settings in Ventura's dialog boxes.

Figure D.1

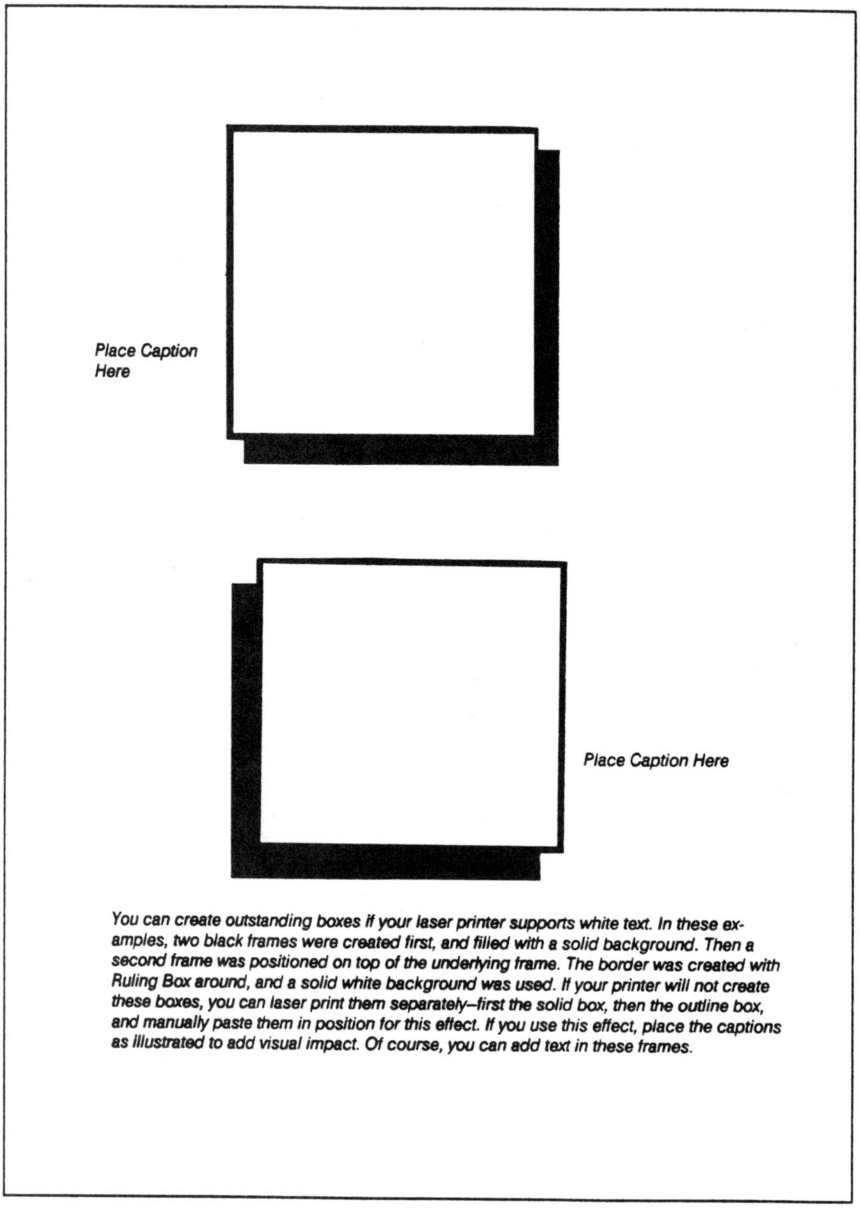

Place Caption Here

Place Caption Here

You can create outstanding boxes if your laser printer supports white text. In these examples, two black frames were created first, and filled with a solid background. Then a second frame was positioned on top of the underlying frame. The border was created with Ruling Box around, and a solid white background was used. If your printer will not create these boxes, you can laser print them separately–first the solid box, then the outline box, and manually paste them in position for this effect. If you use this effect, place the captions as illustrated to add visual impact. Of course, you can add text in these frames.

Off-setting frames can create a very appealing visual effect.

Figure D.2

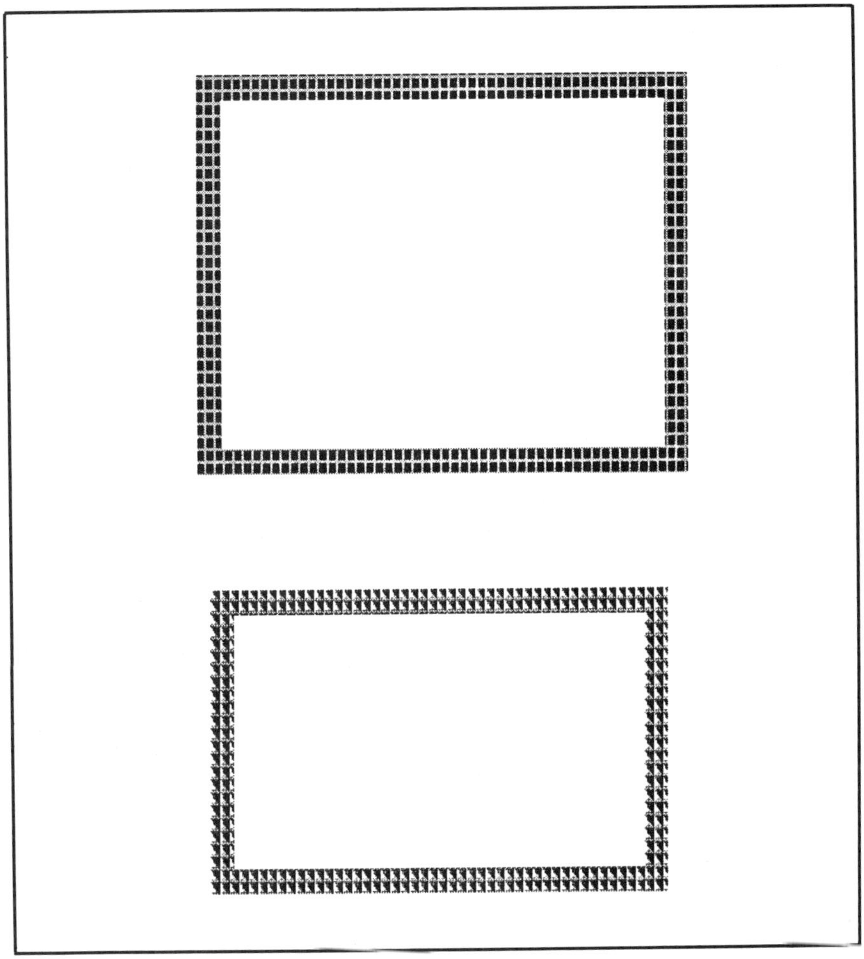

You can create special borders for your frames by using a paint-and-draw program. These two examples were created with ZSoft's Publisher's Paintbrush. A box was drawn in Publisher's Paintbrush, and a patterned line was assigned. The image was then saved and finally imported into Ventura.

Figure D.3

APPENDIX E: VENTURA'S PATTERNS

Ventura Publisher's patterns create special effects for your publications. There are eight patterns (numbered one through seven), plus solid. These patterns are easily selected in Ventura's dialog box.

This figure displays examples of Ventura's eight patterns. They were printed on a standard HP LaserJet II. You should print a similar test document to see the difference between each of Ventura's patterns. If you are planning to use a service bureau to output your Ventura files, you may also find it helpful to send a test document such as this one to your service bureau.

Figure E.1

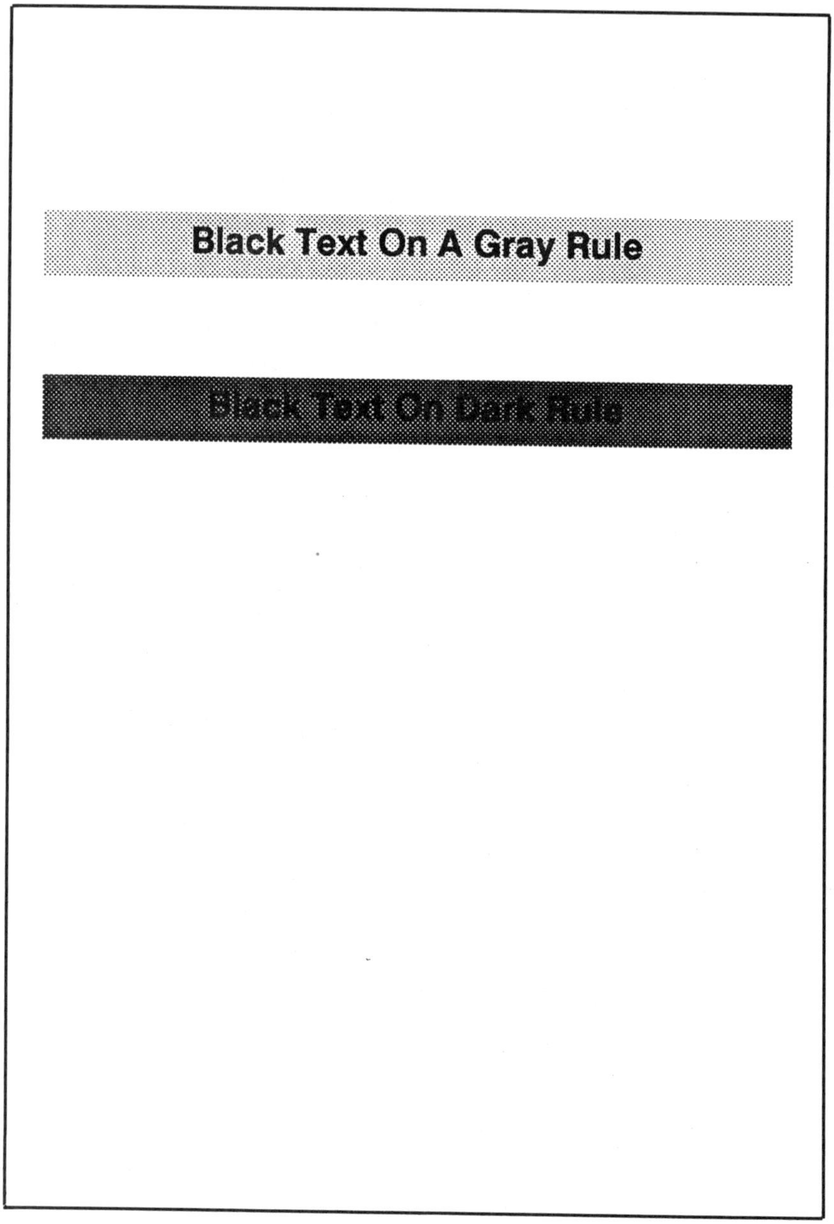

You must be careful when placing text on a patterned, gray rule. As you can see from this example, you can make the text difficult to read. (You can position the rules by selecting Ruling Line Above from the Paragraph menu, and entering the correct settings.)

Figure E.2

micro**Publishing Report**

Small Computer Solutions for Publications Professionals

2004 Curtis Ave. #A   Redondo Beach, CA 90278   (213) 376-5724

March 1, 1986

Mr. Joe Smith
ABC Corporation
123 Main St.
Detroit, MI 43434

INVOICE

Quantity	Description	Price	Subtotal
1	Subscription	$175.00	$175.00
5	Seminar fee including late charges	$575.00	$2,875.00

Total now due: $3,050.00

This figure shows the &INV-P1.CHP provided with Ventura Publisher. You can print this document on your laser to see how the pattern appears. If you are having problems adjusting your Ruling Line Above to print like this example, check the settings of the paragraph tag called Invoice.

Figure E.3

INDEX

D

E

X

Z